Outcomes Research in Animal Health Care

Barbara Poulsen Nautrup

Outcomes Research in Animal Health Care

Applications in Companion Animal Medicine and Livestock Production

Springer

Barbara Poulsen Nautrup
Aachen, Germany

ISBN 978-3-032-12586-6 ISBN 978-3-032-12587-3 (eBook)
https://doi.org/10.1007/978-3-032-12587-3

Editorial Contact: Annette Klaus
This Springer imprint is published by the registered company Springer Nature Switzerland AG
The registered company address is: Gewerbestrasse 11, 6330 Cham, Switzerland

In memory of my sister, Cordula, who inspired my path in scientific writing.

Preface

Outcomes research (OR) has significantly reshaped decision-making in human health care, from guiding reimbursement policy to informing everyday clinical guidelines. In veterinary medicine, OR has also gained increasing importance, offering essential insights into real-world impact of interventions on animal health, welfare, and economic sustainability.

This book demonstrates how OR can add value to animal health care. Using plain language and real-world examples, it shows how to judge whether an intervention justifies its cost, how to measure outcomes that truly matter to animals and their caretakers, and how to balance welfare, public health, and financial considerations. The book is intended for a broad audience, including students, veterinary practitioners, researchers, industry professionals, livestock producers, and policymakers. No specialized background in economics, epidemiology, or statistics is required.

The purpose of this book is threefold. First, it seeks to spark curiosity about the relevance and potential of OR in animal health. Second, it aims to equip readers, especially newcomers, with the tools to critically assess existing work, e.g., to recognize sound study designs, identify common pitfalls, and judge reported outcomes. Third, the content may be a starting point for researchers who want to work in the broad field of OR.

To meet these aims, the book is organized into four parts:

I. *A concise overview* traces the evolution of OR in human health, drawing parallels with animal health care. It outlines the current role of OR in veterinary medicine and explains key terminology.
II. *Core research methods*, including prospective and retrospective studies and meta-analyses, are explained step-by-step and illustrated with real-world examples from veterinary medicine to highlight their usefulness for different purposes and draw attention to their specific limitations.
III. *Health-economic studies* are described, and the usefulness of different analyses for various species, i.e., livestock and companion animals, is demonstrated through illustrative examples.
IV. *Quality of life and animal welfare metrics* are introduced, including the groundbreaking tools from human medicine, i.e., the quality-adjusted life years (QALYs) and disability-adjusted life years (DALYs), along with early efforts to adapt these concepts to animal health care.

The chapters start with the fundamentals and end with "Take-Home Messages" and suggestions for further reading. As each chapter stands alone, readers are free to dive straight into the topics that interest them most without the need to progress from chapter to chapter.

While this book offers a comprehensive overview of OR in veterinary medicine, it cannot cover every aspect of this broad field of research. It is my hope that future works will build on this foundation, filling gaps and further advancing the role of OR in animal health care.

This book would not have been possible without the support and collaboration of colleagues who have been essential in advancing OR in animal health. Their efforts have laid the groundwork on which this work is built. I am particularly grateful to two reviewers who wish to remain anonymous, for their thoughtful comments and valuable suggestions. Any remaining shortcomings are, of course, my own.

Aachen, Germany Barbara Poulsen Nautrup

Competing Interests

The author has no competing interests to declare that are relevant to the content of this manuscript.

Contents

About the Author

Barbara Poulsen Nautrup graduated as a veterinarian at the University of Veterinary Medicine Hannover (Germany) and finalized her doctoral thesis at the "Freie Universität Berlin", Germany. She holds a master's degree in Health Economics and Pharmacoeconomics, granted by the University Pompeu Fabra, Barcelona, Spain, and was docent at the European Business School (EBS), Oestrich-Winkel, Germany. Before founding her own consultancy in health economics and outcomes research, she worked in veterinary and human pharmaceutical companies, where she was involved in the development of clinical study designs and responsible for retrospective analysis and health economic studies. As a consultant, she has dedicated a better part of her work to support outcomes research in animal health care, with a focus on economic analyses and meta-analyses. Her long history of working in health economics and outcomes research in human and veterinary medicine is proven by a long list of conference presentations and articles published in peer-reviewed journals.

Her motivation for writing this book stems from her belief in the power of outcomes research to improve livestock productivity and enhance health care and welfare for all animals.

Part I

Introduction to Outcomes Research

Outcomes research is a comparatively young discipline that has gained great significance in human health care and is also increasingly acknowledged in veterinary medicine as a valuable tool assessing health care interventions and burden of diseases, thereby supporting evidence-based decision-making.

Outcomes Research: Definition, History, and Applications

1

Abstract

Outcomes research (OR) is an emerging discipline in animal health care that aims to optimize the results of veterinary interventions. It considers both the clinical impact and economic factors. Economic analyses have been widely used to support decisions in livestock. Although costs remain a crucial aspect in animals intended for food production, animal well-being, a core area of OR, is also becoming more important in livestock. In pets and horses, quality of life is a critical decision factor. However, in these animals, limitations exist to express changes in quality of life or life expectancy in monetary units. This limitation hinders the adoption of economic analyses conventionally used in livestock. Cost-effectiveness analyses have the potential to fill this gap, as they assess costs and outcomes separately. They can support difficult decisions when costs and the well-being of the animal must be considered. Tools have been developed that allow the consideration of quality of life or animal welfare in health economic studies. On a global level, OR can support far-reaching projects, such as disease eradication programs and zoonosis control in developing countries, by evaluating the broad impact of interventions on both animals and humans.

Keywords

Outcomes research · Health economics · Patient-reported outcomes · Quality of life · Health care decisions

1.1 Definition and Basic Concept

OR and health economics are two closely linked disciplines, and in human medicine the term *HEOR (health economics and outcomes research)* is commonly found, underlining the close ties between the two disciplines. OR focuses on understanding

B. Poulsen Nautrup, *Outcomes Research in Animal Health Care*,
https://doi.org/10.1007/978-3-032-12587-3_1

the results of health care interventions, measuring how they affect the health, well-being, and financial costs for patients or stakeholders. Although the information gathered by means of OR is valuable in itself, the use of these data in health economic analyses can provide even greater benefit, contributing to informed decision-making in livestock production, on disease eradication programs, but also supporting decisions on health care interventions in a single animal.

While many definitions exist, we adopt the definition from a recent article on OR in veterinary medicine: "Outcomes research entails the application of clinical- and population-based research methods to optimize the end results of healthcare practices and interventions, delivering benefits and value to stakeholders" [1].

Put simply, OR evaluates how well a treatment works in the real world and whether the benefits justify the costs. It aims to support the use of health care interventions most efficiently, by evaluating the outcome for the patient, thereby also considering the resources that need to be invested.

A key aspect of OR is the patient-centered focus. Rather than focusing on surrogate measures such as lab tests, OR emphasizes outcomes that matter to the animal, the animal owner, veterinarian, and other stakeholders, such as recovery, health improvement, increased productivity, quality of life, or animal welfare.

When combining these outcomes with costs, OR is intended to support clinicians, animal caretakers, or other stakeholders to decide on the most appropriate health care intervention, thereby enhancing the quality and efficiency of animal health care delivery.

Stakeholders in veterinary decisions can vary widely:

- An individual pet owner may decide on a treatment based on affordability and the pet's quality of life.
- A farm manager may evaluate whether a health intervention improves productivity while maintaining profitability.
- Livestock companies need to estimate the return of planned investments.
- On a larger scale, governments and global health organizations may assess the value of disease control programs.
- In countries with a high coverage of pet insurances, the insurers can decide on therapies that are covered and those that are not reimbursed, based on their cost-effectiveness.

1.2 The History of OR in Human Health Care

The history and development of OR in human health care has been summarized in detail [2], whereas we focus here on those developments that allow parallels to be drawn with veterinary medicine.

First efforts in OR, although not called as such, have been reported in the early 1900s. However, many researchers describe the start of OR in the 1970s, when advanced technology was applied to a greater number of patients, resulting in exploding health care costs, which were not necessarily related to improved patient outcomes. Additionally, medical practices showed wide variations in treatments, their effectiveness, and expenditures. The huge variations in outcomes provoked the need to evaluate the effectiveness of medical practices, as it was recognized that outcomes in daily practice did not always reflect results from clinical studies. Concomitantly, increasing health care costs required decisions how to allocate limited resources best, considering the outcomes of interventions in real life in relation to their costs.

The creation of organizations like ISPOR (International Society for Pharmacoeconomics and Outcomes Research, founded in 1995) reflected this shift toward data-driven, patient-centered health care.

Today, health economic data are required in many countries for listing a drug on formularies, which include those medications that are reimbursed by national health care systems or health insurances. In this context, one of the most influential tools developed in human health economics is the QALY, or quality-adjusted life year. This metric combines life expectancy with quality of life into a single value, helping decision-makers compare treatment options.

▶ Short Note
The QALY-concept will be described in detail in Chap. 13 of this book as first attempts have been made to create a similar concept for animal health care.

Another related metric is the DALY (disability-adjusted life year), which is commonly used in public health and global medicine. It estimates the burden of disease by combining years lost due to early death and years lived with disability. DALYs are especially important in zoonotic disease control, where animal health and human health intersect.

▶ Short Note
This concept will be described in the last chapter (Chap. 14) of this book, which also presents first examples of an adaptation of the DALY to animals.

Altogether, in human medicine, OR has become a fundamental cornerstone of modern health care, linking clinical efficiency with patient's quality of life and satisfaction. Its evolution reflects a shift in the health care landscape toward

- evidence-based practice
- patient-centered care
- value-driven health systems

Therefore, OR can not only improve individual patient outcomes but also enhance the efficiency of health care systems.

1.3 OR in Animal Health Care

1.3.1 When and Why Was OR Introduced in Animal Health Care?

The formal term OR is hardly found in early literature of animal health care, whereas health economic analyses have been used for decades especially in livestock. Starting in the 1960s and early 1970s, governments began using economic studies to support disease control programs. At the same time, the economic impact of less dramatic diseases such as infertility and parasitism has become increasingly obvious [3], and economic analyses have been recognized as an important tool to support treatment decisions in livestock.

Today, OR extends beyond simple decisions on the most appropriate treatment or preventive measure and also includes biosecurity or environmental aspects. While financial considerations are still central in livestock industries, consumer awareness and animal welfare laws have increased the importance of health and welfare metrics in production systems.

In companion animals, the cost of veterinary care continues to rise, and owners are increasingly concerned with quality of life. However, in these animals, limitations exist to express changes in quality of life or life expectancy in monetary units, which have hindered the adoption of economic analyses conventionally used in livestock. This is where cost-effectiveness analysis becomes useful, as this kind of health economic analysis evaluates and assesses both costs and outcomes separately, without the need to convert animal comfort or lifespan into money. Authors affiliated with the Royal Veterinary College in UK literally stated: "As in human health, it is likely that cost-effectiveness will become increasingly predominant in assessments of animal health, production, and welfare, emphasizing the importance of understanding the strength and limitations of this tool" [4].

According with the current and anticipated development of OR in animal health, first veterinary pharmaceutical companies have set up OR departments. Additionally, the Kansas State University's College of Veterinary Medicine was the first to establish a respective center (Center for Outcomes Research and Epidemiology, CORE) in a veterinary college [1].

1.3.2 What Are the Aims and Applications of OR in Animal Health Care?

The main goals of OR in animal health care can be summarized as follows:

- to assess the cost, effectiveness, and outcomes of interventions
- to demonstrate the outcome to stakeholders like pet owners, livestock producers, and veterinarians, thereby optimizing resource allocation in veterinary medicine
- to support decision-making on global or governmental health care programs

The focus lies on striking a balance between economic sustainability, animal well-being, productivity, and societal benefits.

According to its aim, OR in animal health is broadly diversified, and the methods and tools used depend on the purpose of the animal (companion animal versus food production animals) and the target group, e.g., veterinarian, pet owner, livestock owner, producer, consumer, government official, or national or international health organization.

- In companion animals, cost-effectiveness analysis of veterinary treatments provides a balance of costs, outcomes, and quality of life for pets and horses, thereby also minimizing the use of clinical practices or interventions that are medically ineffective or not cost-effective. Assessing the quality of life not only allows for the evaluation of the impact of a treatment on the animal's well-being but can also support difficult decisions when reaching the end of life and related decisions on euthanasia. Although relevant only in countries with widespread animal health insurance, OR can help insurers determine which treatments or preventive care options should be covered, based on their economic value and health outcomes.
- In livestock, health economic analyses based on valid OR data can link health interventions and changes of management aspects to measurable gains in productivity and animal welfare.
- On a more global level, OR data can be used to assess the cost-benefit of preventive programs or disease eradication programs. The One Health initiatives need sound OR data to evaluate the economic impact of integrated approaches to manage zoonotic diseases, such as rabies, to protect both animal and human populations.

Accordingly, it has been stated that the systematic application of valid outcomes research approaches could lead to more informed stakeholders and clients and optimal care for veterinary patients [1].

Take-Home Messages

- Outcomes research evaluates how well a health care intervention works in real-world settings and whether the benefits justify the costs.
- It aims to support the use of health care interventions most efficiently.
- It supports evidence-based decisions, whether on individual treatments, health, or management strategies, or on a more global level, such as disease control programs.
- A range of tools has been developed to address the specific needs in livestock and companion animal settings.

References

1. Cernicchiaro N, Oliveira ARS, Hanthorn C, Renter DG (2022) Outcomes research: origins, relevance, and potential impacts for veterinary medicine. J Am Vet Med Assoc 260(7):714–723
2. Lee SJ, Earle CC, Weeks JC (2000) Outcomes research in oncology: history, conceptual framework, and trends in the literature. J Natl Cancer Inst 92(3):195–204
3. Rushton J (2009) The economics of animal health and production. CAB International, Oxfordshire
4. Babo Martins S, Rushton J (2014) Cost-effectiveness analysis: adding value to assessment of animal health, welfare and production. Rev Sci Tech OIE 33(3):681–689

Part II

Data Sources and Applications

Regardless, if we want to assess the impact of a medical intervention, the burden of disease, the quality of life or animal welfare, appropriate data must be collected, typically through clinical studies and/or desk research. These approaches are the main focus of this part. Clinical studies in particular can vary greatly in terms of compliance. As the adherence to treatment recommendations can significantly influence the success of veterinary interventions, it is important to consider compliance when interpreting results from clinical studies. Given the significance of non-compliance for both patients and stakeholders, it seemed appropriate to begin this part with a chapter dedicated to compliance, describing its occurrence, importance, and its significance in OR.

Compliance

2

Abstract

Although different definitions exist, compliance can be described as the consistency and accuracy with which treatment regimes, laws, or guidelines are followed. The reasons for noncompliance might differ between owners of different animal species. However, the problem affects pets, horses, and livestock. Many compliance studies have been conducted in dogs, including those evaluating compliance with short-term antimicrobial treatment or long-term medication. Clinical studies often use different measures, such as owner self-reports, pill counts, or electronic monitoring caps, which results in different compliance rates. Retrospective studies used transaction data to approximate the compliance with long-term medication in dogs. However, noncompliance can also involve the following of management recommendations or guidelines, as shown in studies on horses and livestock. The presented examples highlight the extent of the problem in companion animals and livestock. Depending on the indication, noncompliance can substantially impact the outcome and should always be considered when evaluating health interventions in everyday veterinary practice.

Keywords

Compliance · Adherence · Persistence · Noncompliance · Transaction data · Pill-count · Electronic monitoring caps

B. Poulsen Nautrup, *Outcomes Research in Animal Health Care*,
https://doi.org/10.1007/978-3-032-12587-3_2

2.1 Definition

There is no uniform definition of compliance in animal health care. In general, compliance describes the consistency and accuracy with which a regimen prescribed by a veterinarian or other professional is followed [1]. Thereby the term "compliance" not only refers to treatment recommendations but also to laws, regulations, or guidelines.

▶ Short Note on Terminology:
The terms "compliance" and "adherence" are sometimes used synonymously, although in human medicine they have been defined differently. Whereas compliance is based on the owner following the suggestion of the health care professional as a form of authority, thereby representing a passive behavior, adherence is based on trust, as the patient is better informed and makes active choices on its behalf [2]. In the last decades, there has been a trend in human publications to switch from compliance to adherence. However, we will use the term compliance here throughout the book as synonym for both situations, as it is more common in veterinary medicine. Of course, compliance based on understanding and trust can always be regarded as more desirable and promising than the blind following of instructions.

However, there is another term, found in the same context, i.e., persistence. Persistence focuses on how long a patient continues taking a prescribed therapy. In other words, while "compliance" or "adherence" looks at how consistently each dose is taken as prescribed, persistence looks at whether the patient remains on therapy over the recommended duration.

2.2 Implications of Noncompliance

2.2.1 What Are the General Implications of Noncompliance?

Compliance to treatment recommendations or guidelines can determine the success of an intervention and the outcome for the patient. The consequences of noncompliance can be multifaceted. For example, noncompliance can lead to an inadequate response to treatment, which not only represents a potential risk for the well-being and productivity of the animal, but can also impair the relationship between the veterinarian and animal care taker. Adverse events may occur, if the animal owner tries to catch up missing doses at a later time. Skipped doses of antibiotics can foster antimicrobial resistance with possible public health implications. In livestock, noncompliance can have far-reaching consequences, not only for the animals, but also for the farm or enterprise if laws or regulations are disregarded.

2.2.2 How Are Noncompliance and OR Linked?

Outcomes from clinical studies with a strict patient management and monitoring can highly deviate from real-world outcomes, especially because of noncompliance in daily routine. A situation that is described by the terms "efficacy" and "effectiveness." Efficacy is the outcome in clinical trials with a strict patient management, whereas effectiveness refers to the outcome in daily practice, thereby also accounting for noncompliance and other aspects. The difference between efficacy and effectiveness will be described in more detail in Chap. 3.

When noncompliance is ignored in health-economic studies, results may be overly optimistic or even misleading with regard to the outcome in daily practice.

2.3 Compliance in Pets

2.3.1 What Do We Know About Noncompliance in Pets?

In 2018, Wareham and co-authors published a systematic review on compliance in dogs and cats with pharmaceutical medication. Only 8 studies were found, which met the inclusion criteria, and the majority (5/8) of studies examined compliance with short-term antimicrobial treatments in dogs. The authors concluded that the available evidence regarding compliance in cats and dogs was scarce and according to their assessment of poor quality [1].

A study estimated the noncompliance with prescribed oral or topical medication in dogs in New Zealand. Nearly one half (47%) of the dog owners were not fully compliant with the medication instructions [3]. Other studies evaluated the purchase compliance with heartworm preventive medication in dogs in the USA. Box 2.1 provides some background information on the problem, as well as some sobering results regarding the compliance with medication to prevent a potentially fatal disease [4, 5].

Although not being exhaustive, these examples highlight the scale of the problem of noncompliance.

2.3.2 How to Measure Compliance in Small Animal Clinics?

The owner's self-report of missing doses represents the simplest method that can be easily integrated into the conversation between owner and veterinarian. But it also represents the most unreliable method, as pet owners might deliberately or unintentionally overestimate compliance. Self-reports of compliance often need to be questioned, whereas self-reports of noncompliance can be trusted more [7]. However, veterinarian prediction has shown to be similarly uncertain.

Box 2.1: Heartworm Infection in Dogs in the USA: Background and Compliance with Preventive Medication

- The American Heartworm Society has summarized the problem of heartworm infection in dogs in the USA as follows:
  - The causative agent of heartworm disease is the parasitic nematode *Dirofilaria immitis*
  - Heartworm disease is a potentially life-threatening disease, caused by adult worms in the pulmonary vasculature and heart
  - Heartworm infection has been diagnosed in all 50 US states
  - The therapy of heartworm disease is lengthy and costly and often disappointing
  - Therefore, the main focus relies on the prevention of heartworm disease, i.e., preventing the development of adult worms by using macrocyclic lactones, a class of antiparasitic drugs that are highly effective against the juvenile stages of the nematode
  - Year-round administration of heartworm preventive medication is recommended in the USA to protect the dog from heartworm disease
  - An animal can become infected because of the skipped or delayed administration of just one preventive dose

  Source: American Heartworm Society [6]
- Results from compliance studies in the USA, using transaction data from large databases:

Results	Reference
On average, only 25% of dogs received any heartworm preventive medication during a 2 years study period	[5]
On average, dogs which received oral heartworm medication that needed to be given once monthly were on average more than 4 months of the year unprotected, as the average number of monthly prescribed heartworm medication was 7.3 per year	[4]

The studies also demonstrated that longer-lasting medications, such as injectable preventives, can relevantly increase the average time dogs are protected.

▶ Important Note:
When interpreting the results, the limitations of using transaction data for compliance studies need to be considered (as outlined in Sect. 2.3.3).

The owner might also be asked to bring the remaining medication to the next consultation, allowing a manual pill counting. This should be done out of the client's sight, otherwise the pet owner might feel controlled, which bears the risk of impairing the trust-relationship between owner and veterinary staff. However, pills can be discarded before the next consultation if the owner is aware of the supervision. Electronic medication monitoring that records the time of each opening of the bottle containing the medication is a comparably accurate measurement. The electronic monitoring caps record date and time of any opening of the pill container. These systems are expensive and therefore mainly reserved for controlled clinical studies for drug licensing. Although the electronic monitoring can be regarded as the most accurate measurement, it is not 100% free from faults, as manipulations can occur if the pet owner understands the system, or erroneous results can be obtained if the pet owner does not close the container after removing a pill.

2.3.3 How Can OR Contribute to Assess Compliance?

Compliance can be approximated from clinical studies. However, as mentioned above, clinical trials with a strict patient management are poor sources to estimate compliance in daily practice. Observational studies might provide better insight on the problem, because in these studies, the researcher only observes but does not influence the events. Chapter 3 provides a detailed overview of the different studies and their advantages and disadvantages for use in OR.

Another option to address the problem of noncompliance with long-term medication is the review of purchases made over a defined period of time. The data can be collected from clients' charts of a single clinic or from databases including records from many clinics and large numbers of animals.

However, it is important to note that the compliance estimated from these so-called transaction records is the *purchase compliance*, which has some limitations in terms of transferability to true compliance, as listed in Table 2.1.

Irrespective of their limitations, transaction data offer a feasible option to evaluate the compliance with long-term medications, as illustrated in Box 2.1.

Table 2.1 Limitations when using transaction data for the evaluation of compliance

Limitation	Potential impact on compliance
The purchase history of a medication is an imperfect substitute for the number of doses that an animal actually receives but is a reflection of the maximum doses that might be administered	Overestimation if not all doses are actually administered
Transaction data from veterinary clinics cannot capture purchases made outside the veterinary clinic, i.e., do not account for potential purchases that owners may have made through online or other pharmacies	Underestimation in case of purchases outside the veterinary clinic
Purchases might be divided up to other animals in the same or different household	Overestimation if doses are shared with other pets

Table 2.2 The percentage of dogs with 100% and >80% compliance as reported in a study on short-term administration of antimicrobial medication, assessed with different measures

Compliance measure	100% compliance	>80% compliance
Client self-report of missing doses	73%	98%
Pill count	75%	93%
Electronic monitoring device:		
Percentage of bottle openings	48%	77%
Percentage of days with correct number of doses given	42%	68%
Percentage of doses given on time	20%	39%

Adapted from Table 2 of [8]

2.3.4 How to Express Compliance in Pets?

Another important aspect concerns the definition of compliance. Different studies often use different definitions, thereby limiting the comparison of results between studies.

Compliance can be defined as 100% or absolute, i.e., all doses have to be given at the correct dose and time over the treatment duration. However, many studies define a pet as compliant if at least 80% of the medication is given correctly, representing a less rigorous definition. Additionally, compliance rates can also be calculated separately for

- the percentage of prescribed doses given correctly
- the percentage of days with doses given correctly
- the percentage of doses that were given on time

Results vary considerably, depending on the method of measurement and the definition of compliance. An example is displayed in Table 2.2, providing results of a study, considering different definitions and measurements of compliance with short-term administration of antimicrobials to dogs [8].

2.3.5 What Are the Reasons for Noncompliance in Pets and How to Improve Compliance?

The most common reason cited by respondents in New Zealand was a resistant pet. Other barriers identified in this study included treatment duration, inability to give medication with food, inconvenient dosing regimens, number of medications prescribed, and the complexity of the treatment regimen. Also, adverse events with medication, especially diarrhea, was a reason for treatment discontinuation [3]. The development of flavored medications has relevantly increased the palatability of oral medications, which are mostly well accepted in dogs. However, they are usually less tolerated by cats [9].

It has been demonstrated that the time a pet owner spends with the veterinarian can improve the compliance, especially when the veterinarian explains clearly why the medication is needed. Additionally, involving the owner in the treatment plan, i.e., adjusting the time of medication according to the pet owner's daily routine might also be supportive.

However, another reason for noncompliance should not go unnoticed here, i.e., cost constraints. Owners may not purchase refills if they simply cannot afford them.

2.4 Compliance in Horses

In horses, we will use an example of noncompliance with management recommendations. A study on horses with asthma showed poor owner compliance with six recommendations, considering the environment of the horses. Out of 39 owners, 4 had followed no recommendation and the animals did not show any signs of improvement. More than half of the owners (51.3%) had adopted only two or less of the suggested changes. A good compliance was recorded in six cases only, in which five or six of the recommendations were adopted, leading to an overall clinical improvement of the horses, thereby allowing the discontinuation of the pharmacological treatment. The authors concluded that their study emphasized the importance of veterinarians to explain in detail the advantages of the recommended changes to increase owner engagement [2].

2.5 Compliance in Livestock

Two published studies will be briefly summarized, exemplarily describing compliance problems in livestock.

A study on a US swine farm found low compliance for on-farm sow treatment protocols, with only 22.4% of the sows receiving correct and complete treatment during the duration of the study. Lameness was the most common reason for treatment, and noncompliance with treatment was likely to affect the sow's welfare [10].

A study, evaluating the compliance with selective dry cow therapy in Italy showed varying compliance rates at a farm level: the best-performing farms had only 4% noncompliant cows, whereas the worst had 69% cows not treated according to guidelines. Overall, noncompliance was found in 21% of the cows, which were 3.77 times more likely to develop subclinical mastitis compared to compliant cows [11].

Take-Home Messages

- Noncompliance is a widespread issue across all animal species.
- It can significantly impact the outcome of veterinary interventions.
- Awareness of noncompliance is critical in OR and health-economic evaluations.

References

1. Wareham KJ, Brennan ML, Deam RS (2019) Systematic review of the factors affecting cat and dog owner compliance with pharmaceutical treatment recommendations. Vet Rec 184(5):154
2. Simões J, Sales Luís JP, Tilley P (2020) Owner compliance to an environmental management protocol for severe equine asthma syndrome. J Equine Vet Sci 87:102937
3. Odom TF, Riley CB, Benschop J, Hill KE (2024) Factors associated with medication noncompliance in dogs in New Zealand. Animals 14:2557
4. Mwacalimba K, Sears D, Brennan C, Poulsen Nautrup B, Sheehy J, Smith K et al (2023) Retrospective analyses of heartworm (*Dirofilaria immitis*) disease and ectoparasite preventive medication compliance in veterinary practices in the USA. Parasit Vectors 16:149
5. Mwacalimba K, Smith K, Moldavchuk M, Sears D, Brennan C (2022) The compliance and revenue benefits of ProHeart vs monthly heartworm disease preventives in the US. PLoS One 17(8):e0271058
6. American Heartworm Society (2024) Canine Heartworm Guidelines. https://www.heartwormsociety.org/veterinary-resources/american-heartworm-society-guidelines. Accessed 26 Apr 2025
7. Stirratt MJ, Dunbar-Jacob J, Crane HM, Simoni JM, Czajkowski S, Hilliard ME et al (2015) Self-report measures of medication adherence behavior: recommendations on optimal use. TBM 5:470–482
8. Adams VJ, Campbell JR, Waldner CL, Dowling PM, Shmon CL (2005) Evaluation of client compliance with short-term administration of antimicrobials to dogs. J Am Vet Med Assoc 226:567–574
9. Adenot CC, Abdelhakim HE (2022) Palatability assessment of oral dosage forms for companion animals: a systematic review. J Drug Deliv Sci Technol 77:103841
10. Campler MR, Cox JL, Walker HL, Arruda AG (2021) Description of on-farm treatment compliance and risk factors for culling in sows. Porc Health Manag 7:59
11. Guadagnini M, Gogna C, Tolasi C, Tolasi G, Gnali G, Freu G et al (2023) Approach to selective dry cow therapy in early adopter Italian dairy farms: why compliance is so important. Animals 13:3485

Primary Data Sources

3

Abstract

Primary data sources, by definition, are clinical studies designed to generate new information. Different types of studies exist to meet various research objectives, making them valuable tools in outcomes research (OR). Randomized-controlled trials (RCTs) are regarded as the gold standard of experimental studies due to their high internal validity. This makes them particularly suitable for the development phase of new pharmaceuticals, where demonstrating efficacy and safety for marketing authorization is crucial. However, strict patient management, rigorous inclusion and exclusion criteria, and the use of surrogate parameters can limit their use in OR, and results might not reflect outcomes in everyday clinical practice. Observational studies, such as post-marketing surveillance studies, rank below RCTs on the evidence hierarchy but can offer important insights into real-world effectiveness. These studies assess how treatments perform under routine conditions and capture safety data from broader and more diverse populations. Among observational studies, prospective cohort studies are particularly useful for examining how risk factors influence health outcomes over time. Cross-sectional studies, by contrast, provide a "snapshot" of health conditions, risk factors, or disease prevalence at a single point in time.

Keywords

Experimental clinical study · Randomized controlled trial · Piggyback evaluation · Cross-over trial · Cluster randomized trial · Observational study · Cross-sectional study · Cohort study · Efficacy · Effectiveness

B. Poulsen Nautrup, *Outcomes Research in Animal Health Care*,
https://doi.org/10.1007/978-3-032-12587-3_3

Prospective clinical studies are essential in outcomes research (OR) because they generate new data. The studies can be broadly divided into two main types: experimental and observational studies. Results must always be interpreted considering the type of study. In experimental studies, the researcher actively intervenes by assigning treatments and managing events. Randomized controlled trials (RCTs) are the gold standard within this group. In contrast, in observational studies, the researcher simply observes outcomes without influencing them. The different types of studies answer different research questions, which we will explore throughout this chapter.

3.1 Experimental Studies: Randomized Controlled Trials (RCTs)

Although experimental studies can also be non-randomized, we will focus here on RCTs because non-randomized studies have major drawbacks.

▶ Short Note on Non-randomized Trials
Non-randomized studies are prone to selection bias and confounding, which limit their validity. If the decision to assign one treatment or another is made by the animal owner or veterinarian (rather than by random assignment), animals of different treatment groups may vary regarding age, breed, severity of disease, or comorbidities. These differences in baseline characteristics can influence the results. For this reason, random allocation is critical when evaluating the efficacy of an intervention.

RCTs are the gold standard of experimental clinical trials, being high up on the evidence pyramid (more information on the evidence pyramid can be found in Box 3.1). However, RCTs can have different designs and have certain advantages and disadvantages, which will be addressed in this section.

3.1.1 What Are the Main Study Designs of RCTs?

RCTs are by definition randomized and controlled. However, there are several ways to design an RCT, with the parallel-group design, the cluster randomized design, and the cross-over design being commonly used in veterinary research.

The Parallel-Group Study Design
The majority of RCTs in companion animals follow the parallel design, with animals being individually randomized to one of two or more groups (e.g., Treatment A versus Treatment B versus Control) and each animal stays in its assigned group throughout the study.

The study design is straightforward to set up and analyze.

Box 3.1: The Evidence Pyramid

The evidence pyramid is a visual tool, ranking different types of studies by their methodological rigor. Studies higher-up on the pyramid generally provide more reliable evidence, though each study type has unique strengths and limitations.

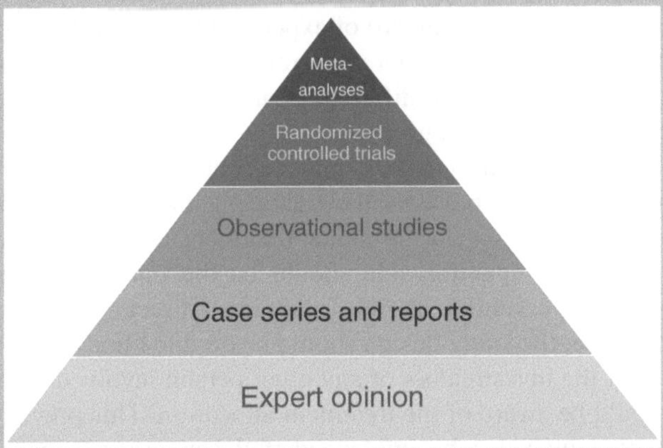

We will not go into detail here about case series or case reports, as they report rare observations, which need to be further evaluated in clinical studies. Expert opinion offers the least evidence as it is prone to bias. However, sometimes researchers have to rely on this data source, which will be outlined in Chap. 6.

The Cluster Randomized Study Design

In intensive livestock settings, cluster randomized trials are often conducted. In swine, it is likely the most common design, with interventions being applied to all animals within a group, e.g., at the pen level. Common examples include vaccine trials. In these studies, intervention effects could spill over to unvaccinated animals that benefit from a lower infection rate if some animals are vaccinated. Trials evaluating changes in feeding practice or drugs that are given in feed or water are also commonly cluster randomized, as individual applications would be impractical if not impossible in many intensive livestock production systems.

The Cross-Over Study Design

With the cross-over design, all animals receive subsequently both treatments. A wash-out period between the two treatments is required to avoid carry-over effects. Accordingly, the animals serve as their own control, as the outcomes of two treatments are evaluated in the same animal. A problem may arise if a carry-over effect occurs despite the wash-out period, i.e., if the first treatment changes the health baseline of the animal before the second treatment starts. To account for this potential interference, the protocol of cross-over trials often foresees that half of the participating animals starts with one treatment option whereas the other half starts with the comparator treatment.

3.1.2 What Are the Key Features of RCTs?

RCTs are considered the gold standard of experimental or interventional studies, as randomization reduces bias and increases reliability. Randomization ensures an unbiased allocation of animals to different treatment groups thereby avoiding any baseline differences between the groups.

RCTs, by definition, need to have a control group, i.e., resulting in two or more treatment arms. One arm represents the treatment under evaluation whereas the other arm(s) can include placebo or other treatment options. When considering another treatment as comparator, this should be the one that is intended to be replaced by the new intervention, thereby allowing a direct comparison.

Wherever possible, the study design should be double blind, i.e., neither the animal care taker, nor the investigators or any other person involved in the assessment of outcomes should be aware of the treatment allocation. This prevents bias in outcome assessment, which can be influenced if the assessor knows the treatment applied in the respective animal, e.g., placebo or active control.

RCTs are the dominant study type used within the developmental phases of new pharmaceuticals, as they have a high internal validity. Internal validity refers to the degree to which results of a study accurately reflect the true effect, free from biases or confounding factors. It aims to ensure that the observed outcomes can be attributed to the intervention rather than other variables.

▶ Brief Example:
In an RCT testing a new analgesic for treatment of postoperative pain in dogs, internal validity ensures that any observed reduction in pain can be attributed to the drug itself, rather than to other factors like variations in surgical techniques, or differences in postoperative care.

3.1.3 What Are the Main Limitations of RCTs in OR?

RCTs are often very expensive and can be time-consuming. However, RCTs also have a number of specific limitations when applied in OR, which are outlined in the following.

Efficacy Versus Effectiveness
The outcomes from RCTs often do not mirror the outcomes observed in daily practice.

The reasons are manifold. RCTs often have several in- and exclusion criteria. The aim is to achieve homogenous patient groups by restricting the inclusion of specific breeds or age groups, or the exclusion of animals with comorbidities. Uniform treatment groups help to find statistically significant differences, as different outcomes due to baseline variations are minimized. However, the groups of animals finally included and analyzed might not mirror the population eligible for the treatment in daily routine.

As a result, RCTs are known to have a comparably low external validity. External validity, or generalizability, refers to the extent to which the results of a study can be applied to broader populations or different settings outside the specific trial conditions.

▶ Brief Example:
In our example of a new analgesic for treatment of postoperative pain in dogs, external validity might be low, if the trial only includes dogs of a specific breed or age, or takes place in a highly controlled clinical setting, as findings may not be fully applicable to a wider range of dog breeds, ages, or less controlled settings, like at-home post-op care.

Additionally, multiple and timely examinations that might be requested in RCTs could reveal changes of the health status earlier than might be noticed in real world, thereby potentially influencing the outcome of treatment.

RCTs also often foresee a strict patient management, thereby minimizing noncompliance. This can be achieved, for example, through multiple visits and strict monitoring, ensuring that treatment guidelines are followed. Accordingly, compliance in animals included in the analysis of RCTs is often much better than that observed in daily routine. Additionally, the often-observed exclusion of noncompliant animals from final analysis in RCTs not only impacts the overall transferability of outcomes, but also represents a risk of bias, if noncompliant animals differ in specific aspects from animals included in the analysis.

As a result, outcomes often vary in RCTs and daily routine. For this reason, the outcome of experimental trials is called efficacy, whereas effectiveness is the outcome measured in a realistic clinical or on-farm setting, reflecting routine care. The main differences between efficacy and effectiveness are summarized in Table 3.1.

Although effectiveness data are preferred in outcomes research, researchers often must rely on efficacy data from randomized controlled trials when no other sources are available. However, this aspect should always be addressed in health economic analysis as outlined in Chap. 11 of this book.

Table 3.1 Differences between efficacy and effectiveness

	Efficacy	Effectiveness
Key differences		
Setting	Controlled setting, i.e., experimental studies	Real-world setting, i.e., use in daily practice
Compliance	Maximized by strict patient management	Mirroring compliance in daily routine
Population	More homogenous, carefully selected sample	Population encountered in the veterinary clinic
Control over variables	Confounder variables are minimized, e.g., by including specific breeds only, or excluding comorbidities	Variability reflects normal patient population
Application of findings		
Question that can be answered	Does the intervention work?	How does the intervention work in everyday conditions?
Usefulness in OR	Less preferably, as outcomes might differ in real world setting	Preferred outcome

Further Limitations of RCTs in OR

Further limitations can concern the stipulated resource use and selected endpoints.

Resource use refers to the utilization of veterinary services. It encompasses everything from the time the veterinary professional spends with the animal to all medical supplies, medications, and interventions, as well as diagnostic procedures. In RCTs, especially when conducted for licensing of a new drug, the stipulated resource use often relevantly exceeds those services that would be provided in daily practice. For example, veterinary visits or diagnostic procedures such as blood analyses, radiographs, or ultrasound evaluations can be required at certain time points, regardless if those would deem to be necessary in daily practice. Accordingly, the resource uses as recorded in RCTs often cannot be used as basis for the estimation of total treatment costs in daily practice. This important aspect will be further addressed in Chap. 6.

In RCTs, often surrogate parameters are used as endpoints rather than outcomes important for the animal and animal care taker. A surrogate parameter is an indirect indicator of another outcome or condition that may be harder or more invasive to assess directly. These parameters often include laboratory measurements or biomarkers that serve as substitutes for estimating the presence, severity, or outcome of a disease or health state. Surrogate parameters are particularly useful in settings where the outcome relevant for the animal and owner is challenging to measure due to costs, time, or invasiveness. Some well-established surrogate parameters include blood glucose levels as a surrogate for diabetes control, serum creatinine as an indicator for the control of kidney function, or fecal egg counts as a surrogate for parasitic load. Nevertheless, in OR we wish to assess the impact for the patient or animal care taker, which would represent life expectancy and quality of life in case of diabetes or kidney failure in pets, or productivity in livestock with endoparasite infestation.

3.1.4 How to (Partly) Overcome the Drawbacks of RCTs with Regard to OR?

With the need of real-world economic data, so-called piggyback evaluations have emerged. Data needed for health economic studies are gathered by piggybacking the evaluations onto an otherwise typical clinical trial, such as an RCT. This approach has several advantages, as the evaluation can benefit from the high internal validity of the well-controlled study, while avoiding the costs of a stand-alone study [1].

However, part of the limitations outlined in the previous sections also applies to piggyback evaluations conducted alongside an RCT. Cost data and other parameters of resource utilization in daily practice can be hardly assessed when they are stipulated by the study protocol. However, other questions might be successfully addressed, such as the inclusion of a quality-of-life questionnaire that is more suitable to be used in health economic evaluations than those measurements preferred in RCTs conducted for licensing.

▶ Short Note:
The aspect of different quality-of-life questionnaires and their use in health economic analyses is comprehensively covered in the last part of this book (Part IV), that is entirely dedicated to quality of life.

It can be concluded that piggyback evaluations are a fund saving method to address open questions, arising in OR. However, the kind of data that will be collected in a piggyback evaluation needs to be carefully selected as it should not be influenced by the study protocol.

3.2 Observational Studies

Observational studies are a valuable tool in OR, as the investigator observes without intervening. However, these studies can be vulnerable to several types of bias, including selection bias and attrition bias. Selection bias may arise if animals are not randomly assigned to different treatment groups, as discussed in the previous section. Attrition bias, on the other hand, occurs when participants drop out of a study, and the animals that leave differ in important ways from those that remain. For instance, in a long-term study evaluating a weight loss program in dogs, it is possible that dogs failing to lose weight are more likely to drop out because their owners become frustrated and withdraw from the study. If these dogs are excluded from the final analysis, the study's results will likely overestimate the true effectiveness of the weight loss program.

Despite these limitations, observational studies remain essential in veterinary medicine. In the following sections, we will focus on three key types of observational studies: cross-sectional studies, post-marketing surveillance studies, and prospective cohort studies.

3.2.1 What Are Cross-Sectional Studies?

In a cross-sectional study, researchers collect data from animals at a single point in time to investigate certain aspects, such as disease prevalence, specific risk factors, or health conditions. Accordingly, researchers take a "snapshot" of a group of animals. This group may be relatively small, such as all client cats at a clinic or a single herd on a farm. However, larger studies can encompass all target animals within a city, region, or even an entire country. These studies are perfectly suited to identify a disease prevalence. Although they can find associations, they cannot prove causalities. For example, if a cross-sectional study finds that cats eating dry food are more often obese, it can state that an association exists between the two aspects (dry food and obesity). However, the study cannot answer the question if cats on dry food become more often obese or if obese cats more often get dry food.

3.2.2 Why Are Post-marketing Surveillance Studies So Important?

As the name implies, post-marketing surveillance studies are conducted after the veterinary product has been authorized. Although animals included in these studies can be randomly allocated, the studies can also be totally observational, making them especially useful for OR. With an observational study design, the veterinarian prescribes a licensed drug or applies an acknowledged health intervention according to the routine in the respective clinic. The studies are less costly than RCTs and allow the recruitment of larger populations. As such, they are important as they can provide valuable information, e.g., regarding adverse events, which may remain unnoticed in clinical trials, because

- they are rare and therefore remain unnoticed in smaller RCTs, but can become obvious when used in a much broader number of animals
- they are restricted to different breeds which are not included in experimental trials
- they only occur in case of comorbidities and/or poly-medication which are excluded in experimental trials
- they occur only in long-term uses which exceed the duration of studies for marketing authorization

Accordingly, post-marketing surveillance studies are mandatory in human medicine for newly licensed drugs in many countries. They are, however, similarly useful and recommended in animal health care [2], although published post-marketing surveillance studies are rare.

Another important aspect of these observational studies is the provision of real-life data. For example, resource use can be assumed to be representative to the veterinary routine in the included clinics. Additionally, observational studies provide effectiveness data rather than efficacy data, as the outcomes mirror the effect of a medical intervention in daily practice, thereby considering the impact of compliance and potential variations in effectiveness in different breeds, ages, animals with comorbidities or different husbandry conditions.

3.2.3 What Makes Cohort Studies So Special?

A specific observational study is the prospective cohort study. Although cohort studies can be prospective and retrospective, we will focus in this chapter on the first type, whereas retrospective cohort studies will be described in Chap. 4 of this book.

A cohort study is an observational study where one or more groups of animals (the cohorts) are followed over time to examine how specific interventions, exposures or risk factors affect the outcome. Cohort studies allow the researchers to assess whether exposure to particular risk factors, such as environmental, management, diet, lifestyle or genetic factors, are associated with a specific clinical outcome [3]. A crucial advantage is the possibility to quantify the risk between the different groups.

In human medicine, cohort studies have been used frequently over decades. In Box 3.2, the interested reader will find a brief summary of a well-known and groundbreaking prospective cohort study in humans, which provides an insight of the potential value of these studies—the Framingham Heart Study, one of the most influential and longest-running cardiovascular research studies in history.

Prospective cohort studies with a long-time horizon and a large number of participants, such as the Framingham Heart Study, are not only time-consuming but also extremely costly, limiting their widespread use in veterinary medicine. Nevertheless, similar approaches are being implemented in canine research. Notable examples include the Dog Aging Project and the Dogslife research project. The Dog Aging Project, launched in 2018, is a nationwide longitudinal study in the United States aiming to identify the biological and environmental factors that influence aging in companion dogs. It collects genomic, clinical, and lifestyle data from dogs of various breeds and ages, with the goal of improving both canine and human health outcomes [6]. In 2024, 50,000 dogs were enrolled and over 50 articles had been published [7]. In contrast, the Dogslife project, initiated in 2010, has a more limited scope, focusing exclusively on Labrador Retriever puppies to investigate risk factors affecting their health, though expansion to other breeds may be considered in the future [8].

Box 3.2: The Benefits of Prospective Cohort Studies, Using the Example of a Well-Known and Ground-Breaking Human Study—The Framingham Heart Study [4, 5]

The Cohorts

- Launched in 1948 in Framingham, Massachusetts, the Framingham Heart Study aimed to identify factors contributing to cardiovascular disease, the leading cause of death in the U.S. at that time. It enrolled 5209 asymptomatic men and women aged 30–62, who underwent biannual health exams
- In 1971, researchers added a second generation (children of the original cohort and their spouses)
- A third generation (grandchildren of the original participants) joined in 2002, along with the 2 Omni Cohorts (in 1995 and 2002) to increase ethnic diversity
- In 2023, over 15,000 participants were enrolled

The Main Achievements

- In the first years, the study revealed now widely accepted major cardiovascular risk factors, such as high blood pressure, high cholesterol levels, overweight, smoking, and physical inactivity
- In the following, the study expanded the scope to evaluate additional diseases, such as stroke and dementia (incl. Alzheimer), thereby also looking for genetic determinants of the diseases

Conclusion

- What began as a small-town study has become one of the most influential health research projects, shaping modern medicine and resulting in over 6000 scientific articles.

A comparable livestock initiative was the Infectious Diseases of East African Livestock (IDEAL) cohort study, which enrolled 548 East African Shorthorn Zebu calves in western Kenya and revisited them roughly every five weeks during their first year of life, resulting in 5337 routine visits. The researcher collected detailed clinical, environmental, genetic, and pathogen data. Biological samples were biobanked and are available for the wider scientific community [9].

However, the majority of prospective cohort studies in veterinary medicine include a limited number of animals which are followed over a narrow time frame. A typical example is a study on pre-weaned dairy heifer calves on 11 UK dairy farms. The animals were evaluated weekly over nine weeks to evaluate the impact of different management practices on diseases in calves [10].

Take-Home Messages

- Randomized controlled trials (RCTs) offer the highest internal validity and are essential in pharmaceutical development.
- Prospective observational studies, such as post-marketing surveillance studies, are generally considered to provide lower levels of evidence than RCTs, but better reflect real-world effectiveness and can uncover safety concerns missed in RCTs.
- Cross-sectional studies provide snapshots of disease or risk factor prevalence.
- Prospective cohort studies offer valuable insights into the relationship between risk factors and health outcomes.

References

1. O'Sullivan AK, Thompson D, Drummond MF (2005) Collection of health-economic data alongside clinical trials: is there a future for piggyback evaluations? Value Health 8(1):67–79
2. GOV.UK VMD (2025) Guideline V: post-marketing surveillance studies. https://www.gov.uk/government/publications/pharmacovigilance-of-veterinary-medicines-in-great-britain/post-authorisation-safety-studies. Accessed 27 Apr 2025
3. Pugh CA, Bronsvoort BMDC, Handel IG, Summers KM, Clements DN (2014) What can cohort studies in the dog tell us? Canine Genet Epidemiol 1:5
4. Framingham Heart Study (FHS). https://www.framinghamheartstudy.org/. Assessed 27 Apr 2025
5. Andersson C, Nayor M, Tsao CW, Levy D, Vasan RS (2021) Framingham Heart Study. J Am Coll Cardiol 77(21):2680–2692
6. Kaeberlein M, Creevy KE, Promislow DEL (2016) The dog aging project: translating geroscience in companion animals. Mamm Genom 27(7-8):279–288
7. Dog Aging Project. dogagingproject.org. Assessed 9 July 2025
8. The University of Edinburgh, The Roslin Institute (2024) The Dogslife Project. https://vet.ed.ac.uk/roslin/research/divisions/division-of-epidemiology/eera/research/dogslife. Assessed 27 Apr 2025
9. Callaby R, Pendarovski C, Jennings A, Mwangi ST, Van Wyk I, Mbole-Kariuki M et al (2020) IDEAL, the Infectious Diseases of East African Livestock project open access database and biobank. Nature 7:224
10. Johnson KF, Chancellor N, Burn CC, Wathes DC (2017) Prospective cohort study to assess rates of contagious disease in pre-weaned UK dairy heifers: management practices, passive transfer of immunity and associated calf health. Vet Rec Open 4:e000226

Retrospective Studies 4

Abstract

Retrospective studies are always observational as the outcome is already available at the time of study. Data can be derived from different sources, including veterinary or herd records, databases containing entries from multiple clinics or herds, registries or databases from national or international organizations. Retrospective studies are appropriate when prospective studies are not feasible, because of time, cost, or ethical constraints. They can provide real-world data and are the basis of most cost or burden of disease studies and have been conducted to answer specific research questions, such as the purchase compliance with long-term medication in companion animals. Retrospective cohort studies and case-control studies are common analyses, which try to find associations between a disease or outcome and exposure. However, retrospective studies are vulnerable to several biases, such as information bias, confounding bias, selection bias, and recall or reporting bias, that must be taken into account when designing or interpreting respective studies. Retrospective research is assumed to become more important, with machine learning techniques allowing the analysis of "Big Data," which are increasingly collected and exceed the capacity of classical analytic methods.

Keywords

Cohort study · Case-control study · Selection bias · Information bias · Confounding bias · Recall bias · Reporting bias · Database analysis · Transaction database · Big data

B. Poulsen Nautrup, *Outcomes Research in Animal Health Care*,
https://doi.org/10.1007/978-3-032-12587-3_4

Retrospective studies are observational by nature because the outcome is already available at the time of study and the investigator looks back in time to obtain the data relevant for the aim of research. Although retrospective studies are located beneath meta-analysis and randomized controlled trials within the evidence pyramid (see Chap. 3), there are many situations where prospective studies are not feasible or limited, mainly due to time constraints and cost or ethical reasons. Additionally, retrospective analyses can be very useful to answer specific questions in outcomes research (OR).

However, before providing some illustrative examples of retrospective studies in veterinary medicine, we will focus on the data sources and the main drawbacks of these studies.

4.1 Data Sources and Sources of Bias

Retrospective studies draw on existing data sources, such as veterinary or herd records (often referred to as "chart reviews"), databases compiling information from multiple clinics or herds, registries, transaction databases, and other datasets maintained by national or international organizations. Because many of these sources contain personal and sensitive information, it is crucial to ensure that data are properly anonymized. However, the reliance on existing data also makes retrospective studies susceptible to various biases [1]. A thorough understanding of these biases is essential for study design, accurate interpretation of results, and transparent reporting.

4.1.1 Information Bias

Information bias is also sometimes known as misclassification or measurement bias. It occurs when data are inaccurate or incomplete. The data sources are usually not designed to collect data for research or to answer specifically defined research questions. Therefore, important data might be missing, including those that have the potential to impact the outcome. Additionally, the quality of data in databases depends on the correctness and completeness of the entries, which is best described by the well-known phrase “garbage in—garbage out.”

4.1.2 Confounding Bias

Confounding bias is another important drawback of retrospective analyses. Retrospective studies often only demonstrate an association but not causation, as an association may be the result of confounding. In clinical studies random allocation is used to control for confounding at baseline, whereas population groups in databases have not been randomized. If, for example, a health intervention is retrospectively found to be associated with a longer lifespan in dogs, this might lead to an erroneous conclusion, if those owners who opt and pay for the intervention are different in terms of their general care for the animal from owners that do not opt for the intervention. Irrespective of this fact, retrospective cohort and case-control studies are often designed to evaluate the impact of risk exposure or health intervention on the outcome. However, to minimize the risk of confounding bias, it is crucial to ensure that comparative groups in retrospective analyses are identical except for those aspects that are subject of research.

4.1.3 Selection Bias

Selection bias occurs when the individuals included in the study are not representative of the target population. For example, animals seen at referral clinics may have more advanced or severe conditions than those treated in general practice, leading to biased estimates of treatment effects. Similarly, livestock in herds with thorough documentation may receive more consistent or attentive care, making their health outcomes unrepresentative of animals in less closely monitored settings.

4.1.4 Recall or Reporting Bias

Recall bias may arise when information is collected based on an owner's memory. This bias is generally less common in veterinary retrospective studies than in human studies, as veterinary research typically relies on records rather than owner interviews. However, when memory is involved, accuracy can vary between individuals or groups of owners. For example, a farmer whose herd has experienced a major disease outbreak may recall and document minor details more thoroughly than a farmer with few disease cases. Reporting bias is another concern, as certain outcomes or exposures may be more likely to be recorded than others. In large-scale herd records, for instance, economically significant diseases such as mastitis and lameness are often carefully documented, while minor conditions may be underreported.

4.1.5 Closing Remarks on Biases

These biases do not necessarily invalidate a study, but they must be acknowledged and addressed through robust study design, careful data validation, or sensitivity analyses. Awareness of potential bias also helps readers interpret results more cautiously, particularly when strong causal claims are drawn from observational data.

4.2 Retrospective Cohort and Case-Control Studies

Cohort studies can be prospective and retrospective. Prospective cohort studies have been described in Chap. 3 of this book, whereas we will focus here on retrospective cohort studies. Case-control studies are always retrospective.

Retrospective cohort studies are also called historical cohort studies. However, in veterinary medicine, the term retrospective cohort study can be found more frequently and will therefore be used in the following.

A cohort study is a type of study where one or more groups of animals (the cohorts) are followed over time to examine how specific interventions or exposures to risk factors affect the outcomes. Researchers start with groups of animals that differ in certain characteristic (e.g., a specific health intervention, exposure to a risk factor) that may be relevant for the outcome of interest. They follow these animals and record the outcomes in the different groups. It is important to note that all events are located in the past. Although often included, a control group is not mandatory as outcomes can also be compared, for example, with population reference rates.

In contrast, case-control studies start identifying animals with a disease or outcome of interest, which are also called "cases." A control group is mandatory, including animals without the disease or outcome of interest, called "controls." By going further back in time, both groups are then compared with respect to an exposure, which has been assumed to have an impact to the outcome. The overall approaches of the two study types are illustrated in Fig. 4.1a, b.

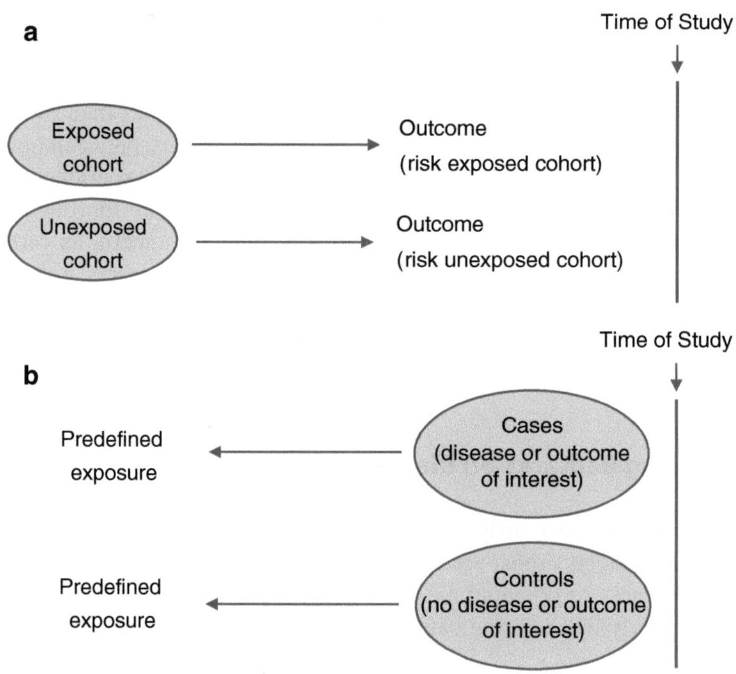

Fig. 4.1 (**a**) General approach of a retrospective cohort study. The cohorts "exposed" and "unexposed" are defined, including animals that have been exposed to a supposed risk factor or health intervention, which is assumed to impact the outcome. Then the outcome between the two groups is compared. (**b**) General approach of a case-control study. The defined cases and controls are compared with respect to a previous exposure, which is assumed to impact the outcome

A crucial advantage of retrospective cohort studies is the possibility to calculate the risk ratio or relative risk between the exposed and unexposed groups, whereas case-control studies do not allow the calculation of incidences or risks, as the total population is unknown. Therefore, results of case-control studies are often reported as odds ratio.

▶ Brief Explanation of Risk Ratios and Odds Ratios:
In contrast to the risk ratio which is easy to interpret, the odds ratio is less intuitive. We will briefly illustrate in Tables 4.1a and 4.1b how risk ratio and odds ratio are calculated.

Retrospective cohort studies are appropriate to evaluate the outcomes in case of rare exposure, whereas they are less suitable for evaluating rare diseases. The opposite is true for case-control studies, as they are not efficient for evaluating rare exposures, but appropriate for evaluating rare diseases and diseases with a long latency period.

▶ Short Example
If a researcher wants to investigate a rare disease, it is often more efficient starting with diseased animals and looking back to find exposures. If the exposure is the rare factor, it might be more straightforward to start with the small group that was exposed and compare it to a non-exposed group.

However, both study types are prone to the general drawbacks outlined for retrospective studies.

Table 4.1a Calculation of the risk ratio for the outcome of a fictive cohort study: from 100 diseased animals, 5 treated animals will die, whereas 20 untreated animals die

	Dead	Alive	Sum	Risk
Treated animals	5	95	100	5/100 = 0.05
Untreated animals	20	80	100	20/100 = 0.2
Risk ratio				0.05/0.2 = 0.25

The treated group has 25% of the risk of the untreated group, or vice versa, untreated animals have a four-times higher risk of death

Table 4.1b Calculation of odds and odds ratio for a fictive outcome of a case control study, including 100 animals per group: In the group of cases (animals with the disease) 20 animals were previously exposed to a defined parameter, whereas in the control group (animals without the disease) only 5 animals were exposed

	Exposure	No exposure	Sum	Odds
Cases (diseased group)	20	80	100	20/80 = 0.25
Controls (non-diseased group)	5	95	100	5/95 = 0.0526
Odds ratio				0.25/0.0526 = 4.75

The odds of disease in exposed animals are 4.75 times the odds of disease in non-exposed animals. This means diseased animals were nearly 5 times more likely to have been exposed

Finally, we will present an example of a typical retrospective cohort study in Box 4.1, investigating the impact of preweaning diarrhea in calves on survival, health, and production. However, it should be noted that such studies are also perfectly suited to assess the impact of lifestyle on the health of the animals, an aspect that has become interesting especially in canine medicine [2], or stress factors on productivity in livestock.

Box 4.1: Example of a Retrospective Cohort Study

The study, reported by Goh et al. [3], investigated the relationship between diarrhea during the preweaning period and subsequent survival, health, and production in dairy cows [3].

The general approach is illustrated in the following figure, using a similar presentation as applied in Fig. 4.1a

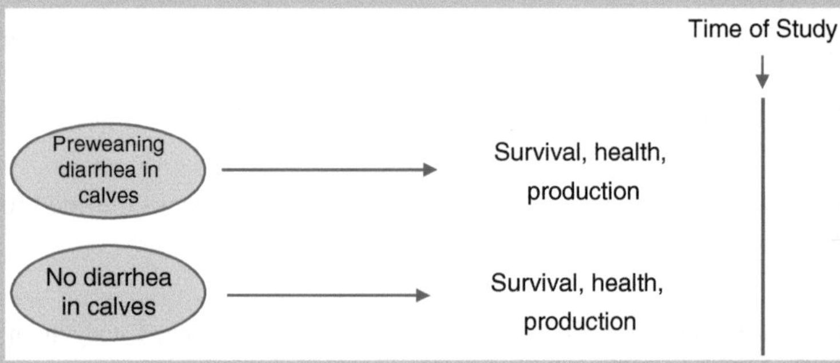

Methodology

- Herd records from a large dairy farm located in Southern Australia were used
- Calves with diarrhea were enrolled along with 2 subjects without diarrhea, matched for age and date of birth, amounting to 9833 calves in the data set

Main Results

- The herd records revealed that calves with preweaning diarrhea had
  - higher mortality in the short and medium term
  - increased days to first calving
  - higher risk of post-calving removal
  - higher peak lactation log somatic cell count
- The last two findings were novel findings at the time of study, and the causal relationship needed further research [3]

4.3 Examples of Specific Retrospective Studies Conducted in Animal OR

In OR, retrospective studies can be particularly useful, as they provide real-world evidence. They can be used to evaluate real-world effectiveness and real-world health-care utilization and costs. For example, the actual utilization of health care services and their costs in daily practice cannot be captured in a clinical trial, in which health care services, such as diagnostic procedures and frequent follow-up visits are protocol-mandated, but would not take place outside a clinical trial.

Additionally, data from different sources can be collected. This advantage is often utilized in cost or burden of disease studies, which are economic analyses that aim to quantify the total financial burden of a specific disease or condition (cost of disease studies) or the overall impact of diseases on the health of a population (burden of disease studies). Both study types will be described in more detail in Chap. 7. These studies are mainly conducted retrospectively, as the magnitude of different data needed for the evaluation cannot be captured in a single clinical study. For example, in a study evaluating the costs of clinical mastitis in the USA, data were derived and compiled from the United States Department of Agriculture (USDA) and other databases, from herd data, literature, and manufacturer's information [4].

Similarly, compliance in daily practice can also be hardly adopted from clinical trials with strict patient management. Recently several retrospective studies have been published evaluating the purchase compliance of heartworm preventive medication [5–7]. Heartworm disease is a severe and potentially fatal disease in dogs, which is prevalent in all states of the USA. The therapy is time-consuming, costly, and often debilitating and frustrating. Therefore, the main focus lies on the prevention of the disease. Several different pharmaceuticals are available for oral or topical monthly application or annual or bi-annual injection. The American Heartworm Association recommends preventive treatment of all dogs year-round [8]. However, noncompliance is the main reason for the continuous occurrence of disease. Therefore, assessing the compliance with the different pharmaceuticals has become the topic of the three retrospective studies mentioned above, which are all based on transaction databases. It is important when interpreting these results to remember the drawbacks of using transaction data for estimating compliance as outlined in Chap. 2. In short, the purchase history of a medication is an imperfect substitute for the number of doses of medication that are actually administered but is a reflection of the maximum doses that a pet might receive. Transaction data from veterinary clinics cannot capture purchases made outside the clinic, and there is also a possibility that purchases are divided up to other dogs in the same or different households. Despite these limitations, retrospective evaluation of clinical transactions can be regarded as useful approach to estimate owner compliance with long-term medication [7]. For further information we refer to Chap. 2 of this book, which is entirely dedicated to compliance.

4.4 Outlook

The increasing digitization has given rise to what is commonly referred to as "Big Data." These datasets are high in volume, velocity, variety, and veracity that exceed the capacity of classical analytic methods. In veterinary medicine, the data are derived, for example, from national repositories or practice-management systems, digital radiology archives, pet-insurance claims, automatic milking systems, or wearable sensors. The emerging discipline of veterinary informatics seeks to transform these heterogeneous data streams into actionable knowledge for research and clinical care [9]. These data repositories provide unprecedented opportunities to analyze patterns, generate hypotheses, and derive real-world insights from routine veterinary practice. While traditional retrospective studies often rely on modest-sized datasets, the availability of centralized electronic medical records, herd monitoring systems, and national registries has laid the foundation for more data-intensive investigations.

Big Data is not just a matter of scale; it encompasses a shift in methodology, particularly through the integration of machine learning techniques, a subfield of artificial intelligence, that can process and model complex information. As such, Big Data is poised to become a cornerstone of retrospective research in both companion and production animal medicine.

Take-Home Messages

- Retrospective studies can be particularly useful in OR, as they can provide real world data for costs, effectiveness, and other parameters such as purchase compliance.
- Retrospective cohort study and case-control study are common analyses, which try to find associations between a disease or outcome and exposure or risk.
- Retrospective studies are vulnerable to several biases, such as information bias, confounding bias, selection bias, and recall or reporting bias, which should be acknowledged and addressed.
- Retrospective research is assumed to become more important, with machine learning techniques allowing the analysis of "Big Data," originating, for example, from national repositories, practice-management systems, automatic milking systems, wearable sensors, digital radiology archives, or pet-insurance claims.

References

1. Sedgwick P (2014) Retrospective cohort studies: advantages and disadvantages. BMJ 348:g1072
2. Pugh CA, de Bronsvoort BMC, Handel IG, Summers KM, Clements DN (2014) What can cohort studies in the dog tell us? Canine Genet Epidemiol 1:5
3. Goh N, House J, Rowe S (2024) Retrospective cohort study investigating the relationship between diarrhea during the preweaning period and subsequent survival, health and production in dairy cows. J Dairy Sci 107(11):9752–9761

4. Rollin E, Dhuyvetter KC, Overton MW (2015) The cost of clinical mastitis in the first 30 days of lactation: An economic modeling tool. Prev Vet Med 122:257–264
5. Mwacalimba K, Wright A, Giannakakis K, L'Estrange R, Nguyen TS (2021) Retrospective analysis of heartworm (*Dirofilia immitis*) prevention medication compliance and economic value in dogs in veterinary practices in Australia. Front Vet Sci 7:602907
6. Mwacalimba K, Sears D, Brennan C, Poulsen Nautrup B, Sheehy J, Smith K et al (2023) Retrospective analyses of heartworm (*Dirofilaria immitis*) disease and ectoparasite preventive medication compliance in veterinary practices in the USA. Parasit Vectors 16:149
7. Lavan R, Heaney K, Vaduvoor SR, Tunceli K (2018) A comparative analysis of heartworm medication use patterns for dogs that also receive ectoparasiticides. Parasit Vectors 11:493
8. American Heartworm Society (2024) Canine Heartworm Guidelines. https://www.heartwormsociety.org/veterinary-resources/american-heartworm-society-guidelines. Accessed 26 Apr 2025
9. Lustgarten J, Zehnder A, Shipman W, Gancher E, Webb TL (2020) Veterinary informatics: forging the future between veterinary medicine, human medicine, and One Health initiatives – a joint paper by the Association for Veterinary Informatics (AVI) and the CTSA One Health Alliance (COHA). JAMIA Open 3(2):306–317

Meta-Analysis

5

Abstract

Meta-analysis combines and statistically evaluates data from different, yet similar studies. It is a useful tool to employ when individual studies lack substantial power, show conflicting results, or when a more precise estimate of the treatment effect is required. Results are typically shown in a forest plot, which includes the results of each study and the calculated overall effect. To ensure robust conclusions, the included studies should be similar, i.e., should only display an acceptable level of heterogeneity, which must be statistically evaluated. In case of high heterogeneity, further analyses, such as subgroup analyses or meta-regression, can help explain the reason. Another concern is publication bias, the selective non-publication of negative or inconclusive studies. It can be evaluated using the so-called funnel plot and quantified with methods like "trim-and-fill." A special type of meta-analysis, called network meta-analysis, can compare treatments indirectly when head-to-head trials are lacking. Instead of a single effect size, results from network meta-analysis are often presented as a ranking of treatments or in tables presenting the relative effectiveness between different treatments.

Keywords

Meta-analysis · Forest plot · Heterogeneity · Publication bias · Funnel plot · Trim-and-fill · Network meta-analysis · Mixed-treatment comparison · Meta-regression · Subgroup meta-analysis

Meta-analysis has emerged as a rapidly growing area of research in the animal sciences. To illustrate this trend, we conducted two basic searches in the CAB Abstracts database: one using the terms "animal AND meta-analysis" and another using "animal AND NOT meta-analysis." The results, shown in Fig. 5.1, reveal that over the

B. Poulsen Nautrup, *Outcomes Research in Animal Health Care*,
https://doi.org/10.1007/978-3-032-12587-3_5

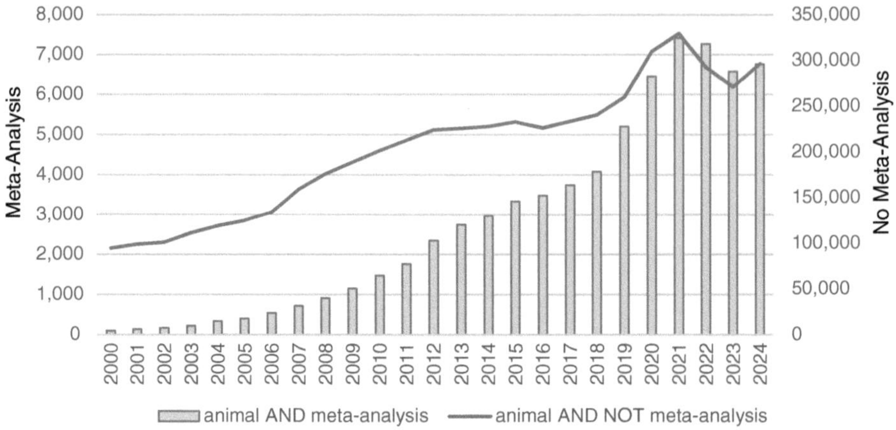

Fig. 5.1 Number of publications found in CAB Abstracts between 2000 and 2024, using two different search terms ("animal AND meta-analysis" and "animal AND NOT meta-analysis")

past 10 years, the number of meta-analyses (represented by the bar chart) has grown to 203% of its 2015 level, while the number of publications excluding meta-analyses (represented by the line chart) has increased to 127% of the 2015 figure.

This chapter will answer why meta-analysis has become increasingly important.

5.1 The Significance of Meta-Analysis

Why do we need meta-analysis when we have good clinical studies?

Results from different clinical studies on the same medical intervention might reveal different outcomes, being beneficial in several studies, not effective in some, and inconclusive in others. Sometimes, small studies show small positive results that are not statistically significant on their own. By combining such studies and increasing the statistical power in meta-analysis, the positive effect might become statistically significant, preventing the withholding of therapy from animals that could benefit from it. Contrarily, examples have also been reported, where non-significantly harmful effects were neglected in single studies, thereby exposing the patients to a risky therapy until meta-analysis proved its harmfulness.

Spencer (2006) defined the advantages and benefits of meta-analysis as follows: "*A meta-analysis can be viewed as a quantitative review of existing evidence. This type of assessment permits data from different, yet similar studies to be combined and statistically analyzed. Compared to narrative reviews, meta-analyses provide an objective and quantitative assessment of available data. Meta-analyses may be useful to employ when studies on the same topic individually lack substantial power, available results support different conclusions, or when a more precise estimate of treatment effect is desired.*" [1] Meta-analysis is typically found at the top of the evidence pyramid, i.e., representing the most reliable and trustworthy type of study, offering the highest evidence (the evidence pyramid is explained in more detail in Chap. 3).

5.2 Conducting and Presenting Meta-Analysis

Various software solutions for conducting a meta-analysis exist, including add-ins for MS Excel, SPSS, SAS, Stata, or R-packages, as well as specific software, such as the free software RevMan from the Cochrane Collaboration or various commercial software (the list is not exhaustive). The different software solutions offer the functionality of the main features used in meta-analysis, while distinguishing by their user-friendliness.

Results from meta-analysis are commonly presented in forest plots, which display the results for each study. The results, which are called "effect sizes," can be displayed by a square or a small line, with the confidence intervals attached as horizontal lines for each study. Considering the results from all studies, an overall or pooled effect size is calculated as ultimate outcome of the meta-analysis. The overall effect size is often depicted in the last row as diamond, with the width of diamond representing the 95% confidence interval.

In Box 5.1 a forest plot of a fictive, albeit not unrealistic meta-analysis is presented and explained.

5.3 Deeper Insights into Meta-Analysis

5.3.1 What Are the Main Effect Sizes Used in Meta-Analysis?

In the example in Box 5.1, the outcome is the raw mean difference, representing a commonly used effect size based on means and derived from continuous data, such as average daily gain, milk production, or blood glucose level. The raw mean difference is the simple difference in outcome with treatment A and B, thereby being quite intuitive:

Average daily gain treatment A – average daily gain with treatment B
= raw mean difference

A prerequisite for the raw mean difference is that all outcomes are measured with the same scale. If the studies included in meta-analysis use different measurements, the standardized mean difference is indicated. It expresses the size of the intervention effect in each study relative to the variability observed in that study. The possibility to combine studies using different outcome measurements makes this method very helpful, but the resulting effect sizes are less intuitive. Commonly used standardized mean differences are Cohen's *d* and Hedges' *g*. The latter has been used in a published meta-analysis, that will serve as a guiding example throughout this chapter. The corresponding forest plot is included in Box 5.2.

If the effect sizes are based on binary data, such as the risk of mortality or the risk or odds of any event, such as epileptic seizures, the risk ratio or odds ratio will be

Box 5.1 Forest Plot

The figure below presents a forest plot from a fictive, yet plausible, meta-analysis evaluating the impact of two vaccines on the average daily gain (ADG) in pigs

Study-Level Results

- Three studies (1, 3, 6) reported a significantly higher ADG with Vaccine A
- Three studies (2, 4, 7) also found a higher ADG with Vaccine A, although the differences were not statistically significant
- One study (5) showed a slightly higher ADG with Vaccine B, but again without statistical significance

Average Daily Gain in Pigs

Study name	Difference in means	*p*-Value
Study 1	42.60	0.00
Study 2	6.80	0.55
Study 3	35.80	0.00
Study 4	31.80	0.08
Study 5	-3.10	0.84
Study 6	36.20	0.00
Study 7	1.30	0.88
Pooled	21.62	0.00

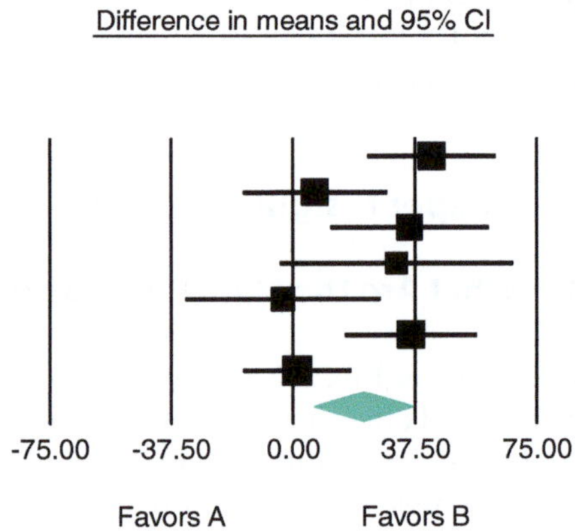

Interpreting the Symbols

- Each square represents the mean difference in ADG between the two vaccines for an individual study, its size reflects the study's weight in the meta-analysis (larger squares = smaller variance, hence greater influence)
- The horizontal lines attached to the squares correspond to the 95% confidence interval (CI)
- The overall (pooled) mean effect size over all studies is shown as diamond at the bottom, with the diamond's width representing the 95% CI

Interpreting the Results

- The diamond lies wholly to the right of zero, meaning the pooled difference in means favors Vaccine A and is statistically significant (its 95% CI does not cross zero). In practical terms, pigs vaccinated with Vaccine A gain weight faster on average than those receiving Vaccine B.
- In this analysis the random effects model was used (see Sect. 5.3.2 for further information)

commonly calculated. The risk ratio is the simple ratio of the risk of the two interventions, thus being pretty intuitive:

Risk with treatment A / risk with treatment B = risk ratio

Odds and odds ratio are less intuitive. Some illustrative calculations of risk and odds ratios are presented in Chap. 4 of this book.

▶ Important note:
The value determining a similar effect between two treatments is
- *Zero* for the mean or standardized mean difference (the difference between treatment A and B is zero)
- *One* for the risk ratio or odds ratio (e.g., if the risk of mortality is 10% with both treatments, the risk ratio is 1 (10% divided by 10% = 1)

5.3.2 What Are Fixed-Effect and Random-Effects Models?

In the example in Box 5.1, a random-effects model rather than fixed-effect model was used for analysis. But what is the difference between the two models?

When using the fixed-effect model, it is assumed that there is one true effect size in all studies included and that all differences in observed effects are solely due to chance. Saying differently, a fixed-effect model assumes that the included studies are similar and no major differences in study design, population, animal management, feeding, etc. exist that could influence the outcome. By contrast, under the random-effects model, it is assumed that the true effect could vary from study to study [2].

In meta-analysis in animal health care, the random-effects model is the most appropriate model when differences due to different breeds, feeding or management conditions or other peculiarities exist, which are statistically accounted for with the random-effects model. However, as a consequence, the random effects model is less likely to reach statistical significance.

To conclude, due to the nature of animal studies and the often-existing diversity, random-effects models have been considered to better reflect reality in veterinary meta-analysis [3].

5.4 Heterogeneity in Meta-Analysis

Box 5.2 shows the forest plot of a study that will follow us throughout this chapter. This meta-analysis is a good transition to our next topic, i.e., heterogeneity in meta-analysis.

Heterogeneity is a crucial issue in meta-analysis. An essential requirement for results from meta-analysis to be transferable and scientifically robust is that the included studies are similar. Therefore, the scope of heterogeneity must be always evaluated and reported in order to allow any conclusions from the analysis.

Box 5.2 Forest Plot

The following forest plot is adapted from a published meta-analysis, evaluating the number of antibiotic treatments necessary to control (metaphylactic use) or treat bovine respiratory disease (BRD) [4].

Study hypothesis was that the reference antibiotic resulted in less treatments necessary to control or treat BRD compared with other commonly used antimicrobials.

The study names have been replaced by placeholders (Study 1, 2, etc.), as the example is meant for illustration purposes.

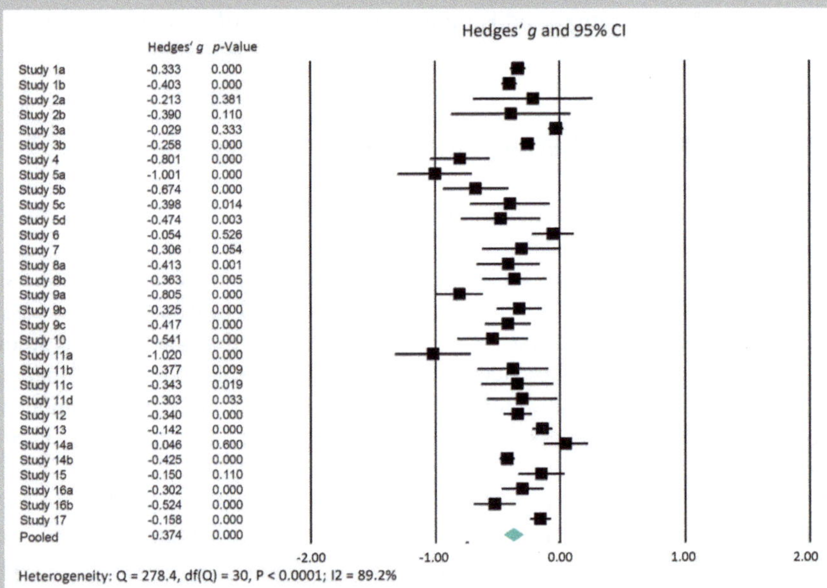

Main Results

- The meta-analysis supports the hypothesis, as the overall effect size is smaller zero, representing a lower number of treatments with the reference drug compared to the pooled group of other antimicrobials
- However, heterogeneity between studies is statistically significant, as indicated by:
  - Q statistic: $p < 0.0001$
  - I^2 statistics: 89.2%, being high according to definition

  (Heterogeneity and its main measures, i.e., Q and I^2 statistics, are further explained in this section).

1. In the first example the outcomes are increasing with an increasing time of treatment.

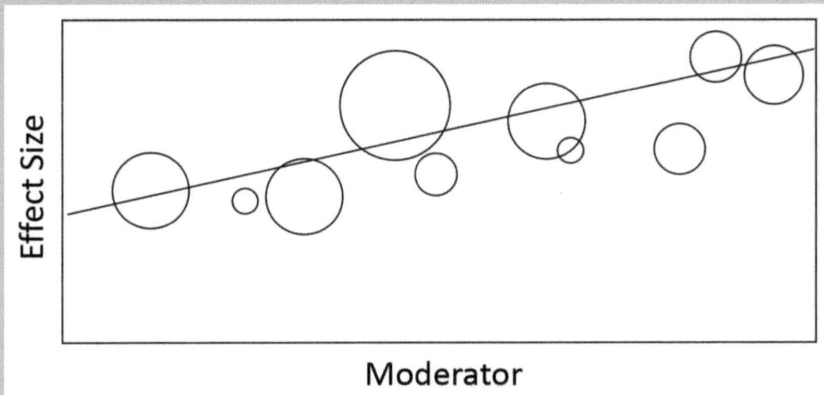

2. In the second example, results are decreasing with an increasing time of treatment.

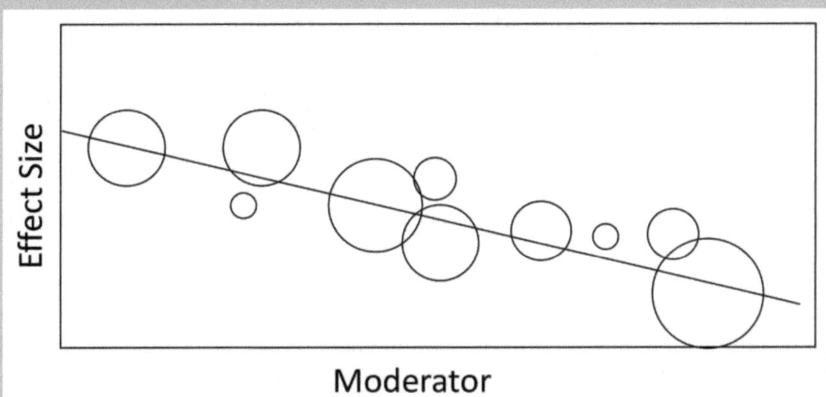

In order to provide meaningful results, an appropriately large number of studies need to be included. Although, no hard rules exist, a minimum of ten studies has been proposed [2].

5.5 Publication Bias

Publication bias is of critical concern in meta-analyses. There is evidence that statistically significant results are more likely to be published than studies with nonsignificant or negative results, negative from the viewpoint of the study sponsor. The problem has been illustratively described in 1979 by Rosenthal in the article "The 'file drawer problem' and tolerance for null results" [6]. Publication bias is

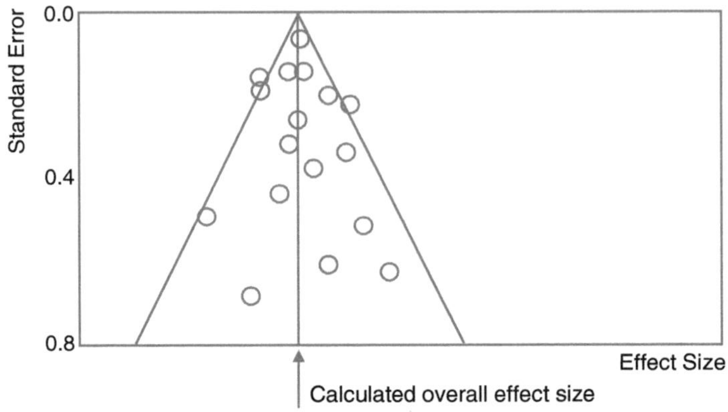

Fig. 5.2 Fictive funnel plot with a graphically assumed symmetry for illustrative purpose

sometimes referred to as "the file drawer problem" in reference to Rosenthal's work, referring to study reports stored in a file drawer rather than being published. Missing studies have the potential to question the results from meta-analysis, if only a biased sample of all studies is considered in the analysis. Therefore, meta-analysis should always include a test of publication bias. Although there are several options to detect and address publication bias, we will focus here on a commonly used method, the funnel plot. It is a graphical presentation that plots the effect size on the x-axis and the measure of variability (which is often the standard error or standard deviation) on the y-axis. It can be expected that smaller studies have a higher variability of estimates and larger studies a smaller variance, leading to the funnel shaped plot, as illustrated in Fig. 5.2.

In absence of publication bias, the funnel plot will have a symmetric shape. This fact is utilized in the trim-and-fill method [7]. In case of asymmetry indicating a potential publication bias, the trim-and-fill method allows the estimation of missing studies to make the funnel symmetric. The trim-and-fill method is explained graphically in Box 5.4, using the example meta-analysis of this chapter.

Another method for estimating the impact of publication bias has been proposed by Rosenthal and is called "Fail-Safe N." It is a very intuitive measure, calculating the number of additional "negative" studies that would make the results no longer statistically significant. "Negative" studies were defined as studies with no difference between the interventions of interest. If the number of additional studies required is quite high compared to the number of studies included in meta-analysis, publication bias is deemed to be of no concern [6]. This method is quite illustrative but has become subject to major criticism [8].

Box 5.4 Funnel Plot and Trim-and-Fill

In the example meta-analysis used throughout this chapter [4], funnel plots were created to assess a potential publication bias, displaying the effect size on the *x*-axis and the standard error in the *y*-axis. The vertical line represents the overall effect size estimate (Hedges' g; random-effects model).

Without publication bias, the number of studies is expected to be equal on both sides of the vertical line.

(a) Included studies are shown as open circles, and the calculated pooled effect size (Hedges' $g = -0.374$) as open diamond.

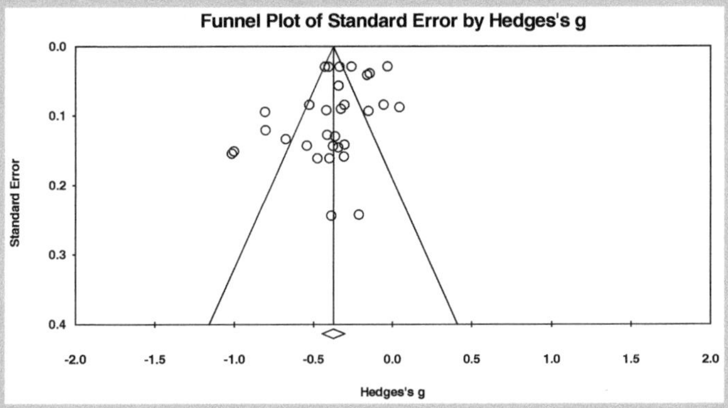

(b) "Trim-and-fill" funnel plot with imputed studies to yield symmetry. Six studies were included on the left (filled circles), making the funnel plot symmetrical. The imputed new pooled effect size is displayed as filled diamond (Hedges' $g = -0.463$). In this analysis, the 'adjusted' pooled effect size suggests a higher difference when accounting for an observed publication bias.

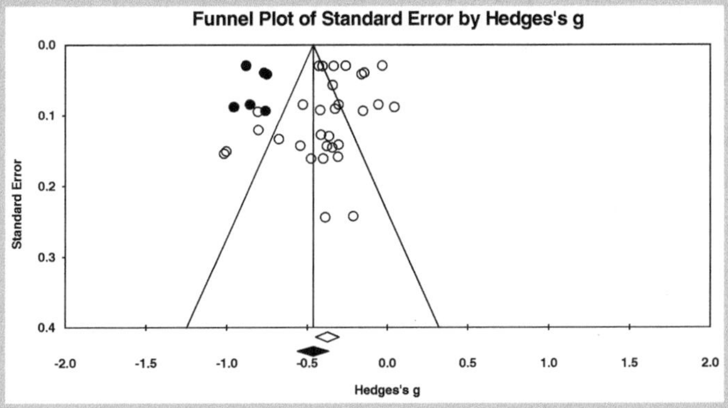

▶ Short Note

In this example, the same size of circles was used for all studies, rather than adapting the size to the weight of study, although the weight of study is considered in the calculation.

5.6 Network Meta-Analysis

5.6.1 What Is Network Meta-Analysis and When Do We Need It?

The classical meta-analysis as described in the previous sections of this chapter requires studies that compare two interventions directly, i.e., head-to-head trials. Therefore, this method is also called pairwise meta-analysis.

However, studies, particularly those conducted for licensing purposes, are often placebo-controlled and lack a positive control group. Even when a direct comparison with another treatment is included, often not all available treatment options are considered in the trial. Treatments that have not been directly compared can only be evaluated indirectly through a shared comparator, which forms the basis for conducting network meta-analysis.

Figure 5.3 illustrates the situation: Treatment A and B have been compared to "No," but no head-to-head trial exists. Accordingly, only an indirect comparison between A and B through the common comparator "No" is possible.

▸ Important note:
"No" in this and the following examples may be a placebo group. However, it does not necessarily need to be a non-active control; it can also represent the standard therapy that had been used as comparator for the new drugs A and B.

Although different definitions exist, the term network meta-analysis is often regarded as umbrella term that includes indirect and mixed treatment comparisons.

In contrast to an indirect treatment comparison, a mixed-treatment comparison includes indirect and direct comparisons. The simplest type is depicted in Fig. 5.4a, also commonly called a "closed loop." One might question why there is a need for a mixed-treatment comparison if a direct comparison between treatment A and B exists. However, the additional consideration of the indirect comparisons can provide further information. For example, the direct comparison between A and B might have resulted in a better outcome with A compared to B, but the difference was not statistically significant. In such a case, the additional consideration of the indirect comparison might further provide proof of superiority, by simply increasing the power of the analysis.

Of course, reality can be much more complicated, as presented in Fig. 5.4b.

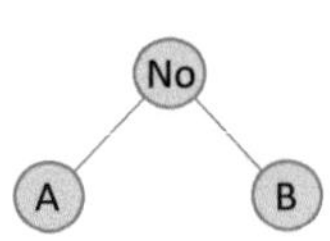

Fig. 5.3 Illustration of a potential indirect comparison between treatments A and B through a shared comparator ("No")

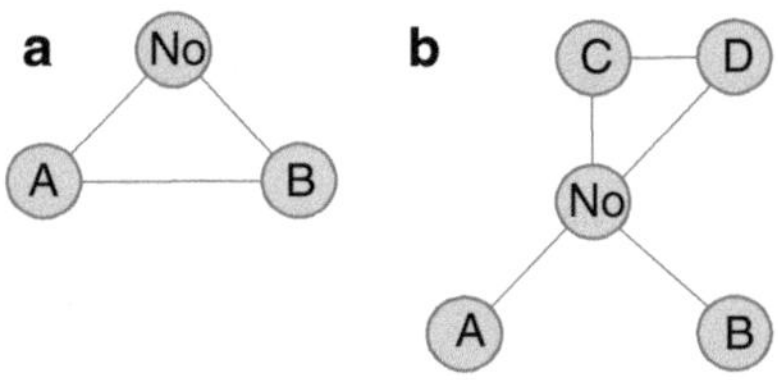

Fig. 5.4 Examples of mixed-treatment comparisons, which combine direct and indirect comparisons. (**a**) The simplest example of a mixed-treatment comparison. (**b**) A more complex situation of mixed-treatment comparison

A situation as illustrated in Fig. 5.4b might not be uncommon in real life. Imagine the following situation: three older drugs (A, B, C) have been tested against placebo ("No") for licensing. A newer drug (D) has been currently launched that was not only tested against placebo, but also against treatment C, which had become the treatment of choice in the past and is intended to be replaced by D. However, if we assume that treatments A and B are still used in daily practice, a mixed-treatment comparison could provide information on the relative effectiveness of D compared to all treatments available.

▶ Important note:
As most published studies are mixed-treatment comparisons, this term is sometimes used synonymously to network meta-analysis.

Although network meta-analysis has been increasingly used and published in human health care, in veterinary medicine only few studies have been published, with four network meta-analyses being conducted for bovine respiratory disease in feedlot cattle [9–12].

5.6.2 How Are Results of Network Meta-Analysis Presented?

Unlike with pair-wise meta-analysis, the results from network meta-analysis cannot be easily expressed in a single figure. Common formats for presenting network meta-analysis results include ranking tables (from least to most effective or vice versa), tables showing the probability of each treatment being the least effective, and risk ratio tables displaying the relative effectiveness among treatments [9]. While the first two formats are generally intuitive, interpreting tables of relative effectiveness can be more challenging. Therefore, we provide an example table along with an explanation in Box 5.5.

Box 5.5 Results of a Mixed Treatment Meta-Analysis, Presented in a Risk Ratio Table

- The following table is an excerpt from a published mixed treatment meta-analysis of studies evaluating the efficacy of antibiotics for treatment of bovine respiratory disease (BRD) [11]. The drug names have been replaced by placeholders (Treatment 1, 2, etc.), as the table is only an excerpt meant for illustration.
- The results are presented as risk ratios, comparing the risk of retreatment (i.e., treatment failure) between different antibiotic treatments for BRD.

Treatment 5	2.84	2.30	1.38	4.44
(1.00, 9.07)	**Treatment 4**	1.05	0.66	1.95
(1.18, 4.51)	(0.31, 2.41)	**Treatment 3**	0.63	1.87
(0.64, 3.56)	(0.12, 1.72)	(0.22, 1.31)	**Treatment 2**	3.72
(1.50, 9.76)	(0.59, 4.94)	(1.23, 2.74)	(1.24, 9.93)	**Treatment 1**

The results show:

- Treatment 5 has a 2.3 times higher risk of retreatment (first treatment failure) compared to Treatment 3 (solid salmon-colored box). The corresponding 95% confidence interval (CI) is 1.18 to 4.51 (salmon cell frame), indicating a statistically significant difference because the CI does not include 1.
- Treatment 4 has a 1.95 times higher risk of retreatment (first treatment failure) compared to Treatment 1 (solid light blue box). The corresponding 95% confidence interval is 0.59 to 4.94 (light blue cell frame). The CI includes 1 and therefore the difference is not statistically significant.

5.6.3 What Are the Main Concerns and Drawbacks of Network Meta-Analysis?

Additionally to the general concerns of meta-analysis, such as heterogeneity and publication bias, network meta-analysis bears two specific drawbacks, i.e., inconsistency and violation of transitivity. Inconsistency or incoherence arises when direct and indirect comparisons produce conflicting results.

The assumption of similarity (transitivity) is unique to network meta-analysis, as in the network all treatments are assumed to be compared in the same trial setting. For example, if in Fig. 5.4b the study evaluating treatment D included a different, e.g., broader patient group than those investigating treatments A or B, which considered only a specific breed, an indirect comparison between D and A or B becomes unreliable [13].

Generally, network meta-analysis requires sophisticated statistical models, which can be difficult to follow, and in contrast to pair-wise meta-analysis, changes in one part of the network, such as the exclusion of one study, can affect all comparisons, making results more sensitive to study selection.

5.7 Data Sources for Meta-Analysis

Last but not least, we will briefly cover the question where the studies in meta-analysis should come from. A meta-analysis should be based on a sound literature review, starting with a search in appropriate databases. There are many databases available for searches of veterinary literature, including BIOSIS Previews, CAB Abstracts, Embase, MEDLINE, Scopus, PubMed, Web of Science, and others. However, limited availabilities, in terms of access to the database and human resources, as well as time constraints might limit the number of databases included in a search. A comprehensive study has evaluated that in case of limitations, CAB Abstracts should be considered in any veterinary literature search, maximizing the journal coverage. The inclusion of further databases would only increase coverage slightly [14].

Depending on the research question, literature published in non-peer-reviewed journals, such as conference proceedings and grey literature, can also be considered. Bibliographies of articles should be hand-searched, and potentially relevant websites from appropriate associations or pharmaceutical companies might also be a useful source. It should always be noted that a search limited to peer-reviewed articles bears the risk of missing smaller studies with unwanted results.

The highest scientific standard for literature searches is the systematic literature search and review. It is a rigorous method that requires a predeveloped protocol with clear in- and exclusion criteria. A strict and systematic approach shall minimize any bias. Sometimes the methodology of a systematic literature search is published in advance of the actual work. For conducting the search, preferably two independent reviewers are needed, who review the literature independently and are also both independently accountable for the data extraction and interpretation. In case of discrepancies at any level of work, an agreement needs to be found by discussion or by enlistment of a third person. This extremely elaborate approach is recommended in order to minimize errors, such as an erroneous exclusion of a study that actually meets the inclusion criteria.

However, available resources and timelines might limit the feasibility of conducting a systematic literature search and review. In such cases, an alternative approach can be employed: one primary reviewer conducts the literature search and data extraction, while a second reviewer independently checks a portion of the work at each stage. This verification might involve reviewing a fixed percentage of articles screened by title and abstract, full-text articles assessed, studies included or excluded, and data extracted from included studies. Any discrepancies should be resolved through discussion, and, if necessary, adjustments to the search or review process should be made [15, 16]. Although this procedure is not scientifically ideal, it can be highly efficient in terms of saving time and resources. Moreover, the often-lengthy process of conducting and publishing systematic reviews has been criticized, as reviews can already be outdated by the time they appear in print [17].

A summary of the main steps involved in conducting a literature search and review is given in Box 5.6.

Box 5.6 Summary of the Key Steps Involved in Conducting a Literature Search and Review

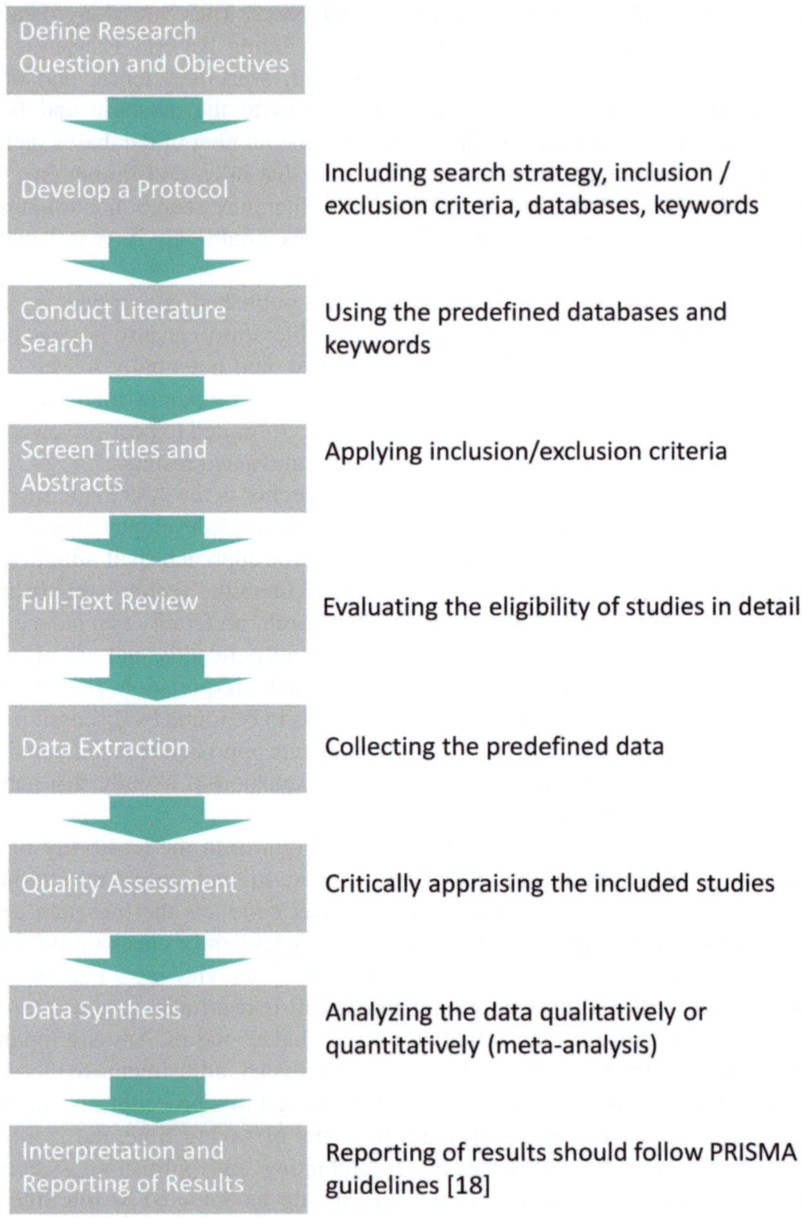

Take-Home Messages

- Meta-analysis combines and statistically analyzes data from different, yet similar studies.
- It is a useful tool to employ when individual studies lack substantial power, support different conclusions, or when a more precise estimate of treatment effect is desired.
- For results to be transferable and scientifically robust, the included studies should be similar and the level of variability, i.e., heterogeneity, should always be assessed.
- In case of substantial heterogeneity, subgroup analyses or meta-regression can evaluate potential reasons.
- Publication bias should always be considered and evaluated using available tools such as funnel plots and the trim-and-fill method to assess its existence and potential impact.
- A special type is the network meta-analysis, which allows an indirect comparison through a common comparator, even if no direct comparisons exist.

References

1. Spencer AP (2006) Meta-analysis. In: Chumney ECG, Simpson KN (eds) Methods and designs for outcomes research. American Society of Health-System Pharmacists, Bethesda
2. Borenstein M, Hedges LV, Higgins JPT, Rothstein HR (2009) Introduction to meta-analysis. John Wiley & Sons Ltd, West Sussex, UK
3. Hooijmans CR, IntHout J, Ritskes-Hoitinga M, Rovers MM (2014) Meta-analyses of animal studies: an introduction of a valuable instrument to further improve healthcare. ILAR J 55(3):418–426
4. Poulsen Nautrup B, Van Vlaenderen I, Decker M, Cleale RM (2017) Antimicrobial drug use for control and treatment of bovine respiratory disease in US feedlot cattle: a meta-analysis of comparative studies versus tulathomycin. Bov Pract 51:1
5. Higgins JPT, Thompson SG, Deeks JJ, Altman G (2003) Measuring inconsistency in meta-analyses. BMJ 327:557–560
6. Rosenthal R (1979) The "file drawer problem" and tolerance for null results. Psychol Bull 86(3):638–641
7. Duval S, Tweedie R (2000) Trim and fill: a simple funnel-plot–based method of testing and adjusting for publication bias in meta-analysis. Biometrics 56(2):455–463
8. Higgins JPT, Thomas J, Chandler J, Cumpston M, Li T, Page MJ, Welch VA (2019) Cochrane handbook for systematic reviews of interventions, 2nd edn. John Wiley & Sons, Chichester (UK)
9. O'Connor AM, Coetzee J, da Silva N, Wang C (2013) A mixed treatment comparison meta-analysis of antibiotic treatments for bovine respiratory disease. Prev Vet Med 110(2):77–87
10. Abell K, Theurer M, Larson R, White BJ, Aply M (2017) A mixed treatment comparison meta-analysis of metaphylaxis treatments for bovine respiratory disease in beef cattle. J Anim Sci 95(2):626–635
11. O'Connor AM, Yuan C, Cullen JN, Coetzee JF, da Silva N, Wang C (2016) A mixed treatment meta-analysis of antibiotic treatment options for bovine respiratory disease - an update. Prev Vet Med 132:130–139
12. O'Connor AM, Hu D, Totton SC, Scott N, Winder CB, Wang B et al (2019) A systematic review and network meta-analysis of injectable antibiotic options for the control of bovine respiratory disease in the first 45 days post arrival at the feedlot. Anim Health Res Rev 20:163–181

13. Ahn E, Kang H (2021) Concepts and emerging issues of network meta-analysis. Korean J Anesthesiol 74(5):371–382
14. Grindlay DJC, Brennan ML, Dean RS (2012) Searching the veterinary literature: a comparison of the coverage of veterinary journals by nine bibliographic databases. J Vet Med Educ 39(4):404–412
15. Wareham KJ, Brennan ML, Dean RS (2019) Systematic review of the factors affecting cat and dog owner compliance with pharmaceutical treatment recommendations. Vet Rec 184(5):154
16. Poulsen Nautrup B, Van Vlaenderen I, Mah C, Angulo J (2021) Do high levels of maternally derived antibodies interfere with the vaccination of piglets against porcine circovirus type 2? A literature review and data analysis. Vaccine 9:923
17. Beller EM, Chen JKH, Wang ULH, Glasziou PP (2013) Are systematic reviews up-to-date at the time of publication? Syst Rev 2:36
18. Page MJ, McKenzie JE, Bossuyt PM, Boutron I, Hoffmann TC, Mulrow CD et al (2021) The PRISMA 2020 statement: an updated guideline for reporting systematic reviews. BMJ 372:n71

Part III

Health Economic Studies

While clinical studies and desk research provide valuable information on their own, integrating their findings into health economic analyses can offer additional benefits. When conducted properly, these analyses can support decisions on health care interventions in a single animal, on a farm or business level in livestock, or on national or global disease control programs.

This part describes non-comparative and comparative economic studies. The latter are often called full economic analyses and include cost-minimization, cost-benefit, cost-effectiveness, and cost-utility analyses. While full economic studies assess which health intervention provides the best value for money, non-comparative studies focus on estimating the economic burden of a disease or health issue.

Cost data are central to any economic evaluation. Accordingly, the opening chapter focuses on costs and related essential aspects that are needed to ensure analyses are both accurate and impactful.

Cost Data in Health Economic Studies

6

Abstract

Cost data are a fundamental component of health economic analyses, consisting of two core elements: the quantity of resources used (such as veterinary visits) and the unit price of those resources (e.g., the cost per visit). While total treatment costs may sometimes be available, the micro-costing approach, i.e., estimating each component of resource use and then applying corresponding unit prices, is widely considered the most accurate method. Unit prices can be obtained from sources such as statistical databases, agricultural records, tariff lists, pharmaceutical price lists, and other published sources. However, determining resource use is often more challenging. The types of cost data that need to be collected depend on the perspective of the analysis. The societal perspective, which considers all costs and benefits, is the broadest and is particularly relevant for decisions on global animal health programs. For individual treatment decisions, the perspective of the animal owner or herd manager is typically more appropriate. Historical prices require inflation adjustment, and costs that accrue in following years need to be discounted to the present value. A conservative approach, i.e., biasing uncertain cost data in disfavor for the intervention of interest enhances credibility.

Keywords

Resource use · Direct costs · Indirect costs · Discounting · Inflation adjustment · Perspective · Delphi panel · Bottom-up costing · Micro-costing · Top-down costing

B. Poulsen Nautrup, *Outcomes Research in Animal Health Care*,
https://doi.org/10.1007/978-3-032-12587-3_6

6.1 Cost Data: The Basic Concept

By definition, cost data play a fundamental role in health economic studies. Costs are composed of two fundamental components: the *resource use* and the *unit cost* of the resources. For instance, the cost of veterinary consultations is calculated by multiplying the number of visits (resource use) by the fee charged per visit (unit price). In cost-benefit analysis, which will be discussed in detail in Chap. 9, outcomes must also be expressed in monetary terms. Therefore, this type of analysis is most commonly applied in livestock production, where changes in health status can be directly translated into financial values. The approach, however, is similar: if a disease leads to reduced milk yield, the economic loss can be estimated by multiplying the volume of lost milk by its market price per liter.

▶ Important Note:
In many cases, not only do direct costs arise, but also losses, such as the death of an animal or reduced milk yield in dairy cows. These losses can be considered opportunity costs, representing the value of the benefits that are forgone. In the following, we will refer to all such instances simply as "costs," which will encompass both direct expenses and losses.

6.2 Source of Cost Data

In general, two distinct approaches are recognized: the top-down and bottom-up costing methods, which differ not only in their level of aggregation but also in their data sources used. Understanding the difference between these two concepts is important for interpreting published studies or for selecting the right method in a new study. Table 6.1 provides a quick overview of the two approaches, which will be explained in more detail in the following section.

Table 6.1 Bottom-up versus top-down costing approaches

Approach	Definition	Data-Sources	Advantages	Limitations
Bottom-up	Builds estimates from the individual case or farm level, then scales up	E.g., farm surveys, clinical records, expert input	More detailed and specific	Data-intensive
Top-down	Starts from aggregate data, then allocate costs to diseases or populations	E.g., national accounts, veterinary databases, surveillance reports	Quick and broad; good for national estimates	Less precise

6.2.1 What Distinguishes Top-Down and Bottom-Up Approaches?

Bottom-up costing generates cost estimates by identifying and valuing every individual resource item used to treat or manage a disease. This approach can use total costs, such as the cost of treating mastitis, which can be derived from farm records or publications. However, the most precise method is the so-called micro-costing. It is the recommended approach in health economic analysis, although the conduction is data intensive. First, each component of resource use that applies to a disease or treatment is estimated, e.g., veterinary visits, laboratory tests, diagnostic procedures, medication, surgery, losses in productivity, etc. In the following, the unit costs must be determined for each resource use [1]. Whereas the unit costs often can be derived from statistical databases, agricultural sources, tariff lists, drug price lists, and other published sources, the resource use may be more difficult to determine. Resource use can be estimated from observational studies. As already outlined in Chap. 3, experimental studies, such as randomized controlled trials, are of limited use, if the resource use is stipulated by study design and does not correspond to those services which are applied in daily practice. Other sources, such as published literature, chart reviews, etc. can be considered, depending on the nature of disease or treatment. Additionally, questionnaires can be sent to animal caretakers that had experience with the disease, asking about the costs they had to incur for their animal. Of course, these data are often regarded as less valid, as they highly depend on the mental capacity of the owner to accurately remember the situation.

The *top-down costing* approach uses national-level data or aggregate data from large databases or industry reports. These costs are then allocated to diseases, regions, or animal groups based on epidemiological or demographic proportions. This method is less granular and useful for system-wide or national cost estimates but less appropriate for health economic analysis on an animal or farm level.

However, hybrid approaches are also possible, e.g., deriving quantities bottom-up and prices top-down (or vice versa).

6.2.2 What to Do in Case of Missing Data?

Depending on the complexity of the analysis, some data, particularly concerning resource use, may be unavailable or incomplete. In such cases, expert opinion can be sought to provide informed estimates. Expert opinion is located at the bottom of the evidence pyramid, as it is prone to bias (a short description of the evidence pyramid is found in Chap. 3). However, data that rely on expert opinion might be considered a better choice than data based on pure assumptions. However, assumptions may also be used in certain circumstances, if they are rationally and transparently justified.

Expert opinion can come from a single expert, but a more rigorous and scientific approach involves a Delphi panel, i.e., a panel of experts that is consulted in multiple rounds of questionnaires. After each round, the responses are analyzed and summarized to inform the next round, gradually moving toward consensus, i.e., finding results that are agreed upon by all panel members. Although Delphi panels can be conducted in person, the anonymity that can be guaranteed by correspondence rather than personal meetings might encourage honesty and balance. However, due to their high cost and time demands, Delphi panels are not always feasible, and many studies rely instead on the opinion of a single expert.

In conclusion it can be said that often different sources need to be considered for the various costs included in a health economic analysis. It is important to list all costs together with their sources for a reproducible analysis. Any assumptions should be made transparent and justified.

6.3 The Perspective

The cost data that needs to be compiled highly depends on the perspective of the study. The broadest perspective is the so-called societal perspective, which considers all costs and benefits that accrue, regardless who will pay for or benefit from it. It is the perspective that should always be considered in human health economic analysis, although there is no payer who actually takes this perspective. In animal health care, this perspective is useful when it comes to decisions about disease eradication or control programs. Here a global perspective is important, considering all costs that accrue for all stakeholders, including the government, national or international organizations, producers, animal owners and relatives, as well as humans in case of a zoonosis.

In human medicine, the perspective of the healthcare payer is often the most relevant when decisions are made about listing or reimbursing health interventions within a national healthcare system. This can be compared with a program perspective in animal health, which considers all costs that accrue for the payer of a specific animal disease program, i.e., the program funder. The perspective of an animal health insurance company, however, may only be of interest in countries with a high percentage of animals being insured for veterinary services.

In general, in veterinary medicine, the perspective of the owner or animal caretaker may be most important, regardless if it concerns a single pet or horse owner, a farmer, or a company running commercial livestock production systems. It includes all costs associated with a disease or treatment that accrue for the animal owner or animal caretaker.

A further perspective in animal health economic studies could be the perspective of the veterinarian, again regardless if it is a veterinarian in his own clinic, a veterinary hospital, or a commercial company running veterinary hospitals.

▶ Important Note and Personal Appraisal:
The outcome of a study from the perspective of the veterinarian might be opposite to the outcome from the perspective of the animal owner, i.e., the best health care intervention in terms of costs and effectiveness might not be the most profitable for the veterinarian. However, we believe that a recommendation or advice being most appropriate for the animal and animal owner will be regarded by the animal owner with loyalty, which might offset an initially lower income on the long-term. Therefore, we consider the perspective of the animal owner as most appropriate in most situations.

6.4 Type of Costs

6.4.1 How Are Direct and Indirect Costs Defined?

In economic analyses, it is often distinguished between direct and indirect costs. Whereas the definition is mostly consistent throughout the literature in human health care, in animal health economics the definition varies across the literature and some studies do not distinguish between direct or indirect costs. We will present in Box 6.1 the definition used in human health care, which also fits for use in companion animals. For use in livestock analysis, we will present in Box 6.2 a definition proposed by the International Federation for Animal Health [2].

Box 6.1 Main Direct and Indirect Costs as Defined in Human Health Care, Thereby Also Being a Useful Approach in Companion Animals (Figure Adapted from [3])

Following this approach, in health economic analyses for companion animals, total costs consist of

- Direct costs (directly associated with the treatment).
  - Direct medical costs, such as consultation costs, cost of diagnosis, treatments (pharmaceutical and/or surgical), hospitalization, etc.
  - Direct nonmedical costs, associated with the transportation to the veterinary clinic
- Indirect costs that may occur if the animal owner has to take days off in order to care for the animal.

▶ Short Note on Absenteeism and Presenteeism:
In human health economic analysis, absenteeism refers to productivity losses due to time away from work caused by illness, injury, or treatment. Presenteeism describes reduced productivity while at work due to health issues, where the individual is present but not fully functional.

Box 6.2 Direct and Indirect Costs as Proposed for Use in Livestock

Various definitions exist for direct and indirect costs in analyses for livestock. This lack of standardization makes it difficult to compare results, particularly when studies report ratios expressing the proportion of direct to indirect costs.

We will present here a definition proposed for the analysis of animal diseases in livestock, published by the International Federation for Animal health [2].

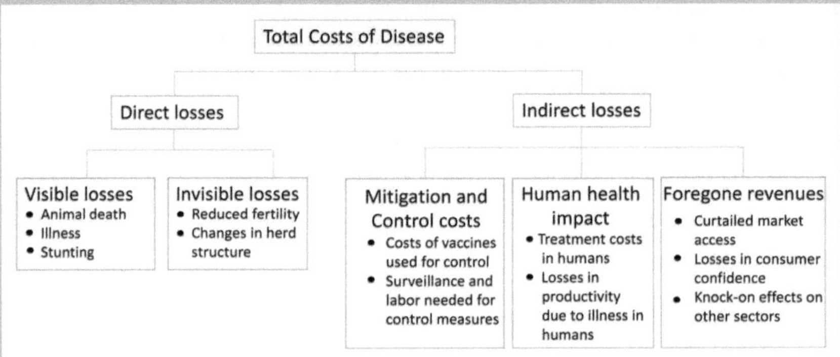

Regardless of how direct and indirect costs are defined, these examples highlight the importance of collecting all relevant data for the disease or treatment being studied, even though not all cost components will apply in every case.

6.4.2 Do We Need to Consider Fixed and Variable Costs in Health Economic Analysis?

It is also generally distinguished between fixed and variable costs. Fixed costs, such as buildings, infrastructure, machinery, permanent staff salaries, insurance, etc., remain unchanged on short term regardless of the number of animals or their health status. In contrast, variable costs, including feed, medications, water, electricity, etc., fluctuate with the number of animals and their level of productivity. In health economic analyses of livestock, fixed costs are typically considered constant and are excluded unless a health intervention results in long-term structural changes (e.g., expanding the herd and requiring additional facilities). Variable costs, however, are usually included, as they are directly influenced by health interventions. For example, treated animals may consume more feed than untreated, sick animals.

6.4.3 What Are Externalities?

For global health economic analysis, such as studies evaluating costs and benefit of disease control or eradication programs, externalities should be considered. A positive externality occurs, for example, if herds of animals are vaccinated and neighboring herds have a reduced risk of contracting the disease, even if they have not been vaccinated, i.e., did not contribute to the cost of the program. More examples of positive and negative externalities are found in Chap. 9.

6.4.4 How to Consider Intangible Costs?

Sometimes you might find the term "intangible costs." This special type of cost refers to nonmonetary costs, such as pain, suffering, anxiety, and stress. In humans and companion animals, these costs cannot be easily expressed in financial terms but have a significant impact on patients' well-being and quality of life. We refer here to Part IV of this book, which is dedicated to quality of life, animal welfare, and their options for consideration in health economic analyses.

6.5 Inflation Adjustment

If costs, derived from published sources, are valid for previous years, it is essential to adjust for inflation, as prices and costs rarely remain stable over time. The most straightforward method is to apply the consumer price index (CPI), which is published annually in most countries. However, the CPI reflects a general basket of consumer goods and may not accurately represent price changes specific to livestock or veterinary sectors. Therefore, whenever possible, an inflation rate as valid for the specific sectors should be considered. That could result in different inflation rates applied in a study, such as separate rates for meat prices, veterinary drugs and services, etc. It is also important to note that inflation can be negative, for example, if prices in livestock have decreased. In all cases, the specific inflation rate applied to each cost component should be clearly reported and justified.

6.6 Discounting

Discounting is a critical aspect in health economic analysis when costs or benefits extend beyond a single year. It reflects the principle that money available today is worth more than the same amount in the future, due to its potential to earn returns if invested. This concept applies equally to future costs and future losses. Discount rates vary between countries and organizations, and rates between 3% and 12% have been used in health economic analyses [4].

The formula is:

$$Present\ value = future\ value / \left(1 + discount\ rate\right)^{\wedge}\ year$$

▶ Example Calculation:
Assuming a discount rate of 5%, costs of USD 100 that accrue after 3 years will be discounted to 86,38 US$ at the present time (100/1.05^3).

However, the discount rate is subject to changes and varies between countries. Therefore, it is recommended in health economic analysis to calculate results for different discount rates, including zero.

6.7 A Conservative Approach

It is always recommended in health economic analyses to use a conservative approach, i.e., using an approach that is less favorable for the tested intervention. Let us assume a new drug is compared with an old drug. Some costs that accrue with the old drug cannot be assessed with certainty, so leaving out these costs would be regarded as conservative approach. It reduces the costs of the old drug, thus being a disadvantage of the drug under investigation. However, using the same approach for the new drug would be criticized as being a nonconservative approach, which might miscredit the entire analysis. We will further illustrate this aspect in Box 6.3, using a cost-effectiveness study, which is taken up again in Chap. 10 that deals with cost-effectiveness analyses.

Box 6.3 Example for a Conservative Approach in Cost-Effectiveness Analysis
A cost-effectiveness analysis was performed for myxomatous valve disease in dogs, comparing a patented drug and a generic comparator [5].

It was stated in the discussion that always a conservative approach was used regarding the cost data. For example,

- in case of treatment failure resulting in the death of the animal, no euthanasia costs were included
- in case of euthanasia no costs for the disposal of the dog were considered

As both events occurred more often with the generic drug compared to the new drug under evaluation, the ignorance of these costs was in favor for the comparator, i.e., the generic drug.

6.8 Sensitivity Analyses

Cost estimates in health economic analyses are often based on assumptions or data that vary over time, across regions, or between farms and clinics. To account for this uncertainty or variability, sensitivity analyses should always include cost data, thereby evaluating how changes in key cost parameters affect the overall results of the economic evaluation. You will find detailed information on sensitivity analyses in Chap. 11.

6.9 Collecting Cost Data: Summary of the Main Steps

Defining cost data for use in health economic analyses requires several steps and aspects that need to be considered. You will find a summary of the main steps required for a bottom-up approach in Box 6.4.

Box 6.4 Summary of the Main Steps to be Considered When Collecting Cost Data Bottom-Up for Health Economic Analyses

Define Study perspective	Decide whose costs and benefits matter, e.g. the animal owner, the herd manager, the government, or the society at large.
Identify Resource Use	List all resources consumed by the disease or intervention (e.g., medications, visits, diagnostics, surgery, etc.). For a cost-benefit analyses also define productivity parameters that are impacted by the intervention (e.g., milk loss, loss in average daily gain, etc.)
Determine Unit Costs	Find appropriate price data for each resource item (e.g., from tariff lists, drug price lists, farm records, market charts, etc.)
Apply Inflation & Discounting	Inflation: adjust historical prices to the present (or target) year Discounting (if the time horizon is more than one year): reflect that costs and revenues in the future are worth less in today's money.
Calculate Total Costs	Multiply the quantity of each resource by its unit cost to obtain total cost for each component.
Summarize & Validate Results	Add up the component costs to arrive at overall estimates. Check your assumptions (e.g., in sensitivity analyses). Clearly document how cost data were sourced and make assumptions transparent.

Take-Home Messages

- In health economic analysis, costs consist of two key elements: the quantity of resources used and the unit price, e.g., the number of veterinary consultations and the fee per visit.
- While unit prices can often be obtained from statistical databases, agricultural reports, price lists, or other published sources, estimating resource use can be more challenging.
- The cost data that need to be collected depend on the perspective of the study, with the societal perspective being the broadest perspective, capturing all relevant costs and benefits.
- For treatment decisions, the perspective of the payer, i.e., the animal owner or herd manager is often the most relevant and practical.
- If cost data are not current or the analysis spans multiple years, adjustments for inflation and discounting of future costs and benefits should be applied.

References

1. Drummond MF, Sculpher MJ, Claxton K, Stoddart GL, Torrance GW (2015) Methods for the economic evaluation of health care programmes, 4th edn. Oxford University Press, New York
2. Oxford Analytica (2012) The cost of animal disease. International Federation for Animal Health. https://healthforanimals.org/resources/publications/publications/white-paper-the-costs-of-animal-disease/. Assessed 02 May 2025
3. Fautrel B, Boonen A, De Wit M, Grimm S, Joore M, Guillemin F (2020) Cost assessment of health interventions and diseases. RMD Open 6:e001287
4. Rushton J, Gilbert W, Jones D (2018) A guide – introduction to the use of cost-effectiveness analysis in animal health. https://www.gf-tads.org/fileadmin/user_upload/gf-tads/docs/document_about/Global/CEA_Guide_Aug_2018.pdf. Assessed 02 May 2025
5. Poulsen Nautrup B, VanVlaenderen I, Poulsen Nautrup C (2010) Pharmacoeconomic evaluation of the treatment of myxomatous mitral valve disease in dogs in Germany. Kleintierprax 55(4):184–195

7 Non-comparative Health Economic Studies

Abstract

Cost of disease and burden of disease studies are two important non-comparative study types in veterinary health economics. While sometimes treated as interchangeable, they differ in focus and scope. Cost of disease studies estimate the economic impact of diseases, either at the individual (per-case) or population level. In contrast, burden of disease studies adopts a broader perspective, quantifying the overall effect of diseases on animal populations by considering both frequency and outcomes, including economic, health-related, social, and environmental aspects. An example of a per-case cost of disease study in dairy cattle identified displaced abomasum as the costliest condition, followed by mastitis and lameness. However, a burden of disease study ranked mastitis higher due to its greater incidence, highlighting how disease frequency influences total burden. The Global Burden of Animal Diseases program is a major international initiative aiming to systematically assess the burden of animal diseases, particularly in low- and middle-income countries. By providing a comprehensive understanding of disease-related impacts, such studies support evidence-based decisions, helping prioritize diseases, guide policy, and justify investments in control or eradication efforts.

Keywords

Cost of illness · Cost of disease · Burden of disease · Global burden of animal diseases · Disease eradication · Animal health loss envelope · Comorbidity adjustment

B. Poulsen Nautrup, *Outcomes Research in Animal Health Care*,
https://doi.org/10.1007/978-3-032-12587-3_7

Non-comparative studies are often referred to as partial economic evaluations, because they do not compare alternative interventions. In contrast, full economic evaluations, such as cost-minimization, cost-benefit, and cost-effectiveness analyses, explicitly compare alternatives and will be described in the next chapters (Chaps. 8, 9 and 10). While full economic studies aim to evaluate which health intervention offers the best value for money, non-comparative studies tell us the economic impact of a disease or health issue.

This chapter describes two non-comparative approaches widely used in veterinary medicine, the cost of disease and burden of disease studies, and closes with another non-comparative method: the cost analysis of a disease-eradication program.

7.1 Cost of Disease and Burden of Disease Studies

Although cost of disease and burden of disease studies are sometimes considered the same, they serve different purposes and may apply different methodologies.

Cost of disease studies estimate the direct and indirect economic costs associated with a particular disease. These costs may include veterinary expenses, production losses, discarded products, culling, and labor. The studies can be reported on a per-case basis or extrapolated to the population level, e.g., the herd, region, or country.

Burden of disease studies look at the overall impact a disease has on an animal population, whether at the farm, regional, national, or global level. They usually consider information on how common the disease is (prevalence or incidence), evaluate its costs in terms of losses (loss of animal or productivity), costs of treatment or prevention, and also consider social or environmental effects, if applicable. Their main purpose is to help decision-makers understand which diseases cause the most harm and should be given the most attention.

We will illustrate the two study types using examples from the same disease area, i.e., diseases in dairy cattle.

▶ Important Note:
Incidence, productivity, prices, and costs can vary greatly between countries and even regions, thereby limiting the transferability of results across countries or regions. Even on a local level, costs can change as new treatment or control strategies might emerge, highlighting the need for regular updates to existing analyses [1].

7.1.1 Cost of Disease Study: An Example from Dairy Cattle

Cost of disease studies are known in human medicine as cost-of-illness studies. In livestock, they have been commonly conducted to quantify the economic impact of various diseases and treatments in different animals and production systems.

Our example study evaluates the costs of dairy cattle diseases. The study published by Liang et al. (2017) estimated US dairy disease costs, using a simulation model [2]. The authors estimated the costs of seven common clinical diseases in dairy cows in the USA: mastitis, lameness, metritis, retained placenta, left-displaced abomasum, ketosis, and hypocalcemia. They grouped total disease costs into seven categories: veterinary and treatment costs, milk production decrease, culling cost, discarded milk due to antibiotic use, death loss, cost of extended days open, and labor costs. The results revealed that left-displaced abomasum caused highest costs, followed by clinical mastitis and lameness [2].

This example is a cost of disease study, estimating the results on a per-case basis. However, most costly diseases on a per case basis may not constitute the greatest burden at the population level if their prevalence is low, as shown in our example of a burden of disease study.

7.1.2 Burden of Disease Study: Another Example from Dairy Cattle

To compare the two approaches, this section again focusses on dairy cattle diseases. Many studies have investigated the costs of dairy cattle diseases on a farm, region, or country level. However, a recent study estimated the global costs and losses of 12 dairy cattle diseases in 183 milk-producing countries. Subclinical ketosis, clinical, and subclinical mastitis were globally the costliest diseases modeled when considering not only their economic impact on production but also their prevalence or incidence in the various countries [3]. We will present the study in more detail in Box 7.1. The study was part of the Global Burden of Animal Disease program, which is described further in the next section (Sect. 7.1.3). In this context, the authors developed a method to adjust for comorbidities. It has been shown that several diseases in dairy cows predispose for other dairy diseases. Analyzing each condition in isolation, without accounting for their predisposing effects, could lead to an overestimation of the total burden.

Box 7.1 Burden of Disease Study: Global Losses Due to Dairy Cattle Diseases, as Reported by Rasmussen et al. (2024) [3]

The authors used an economic simulation model to estimate the global impact of 12 dairy cattle diseases in 183 milk-producing countries. Results were calculated for six continental regions (Africa, Asia, Europe, Latin America, North America, Oceania) and summarized in a global burden of disease estimate. The in-put data included

- Country-level input values, such as prices (milk price, replacement price, culled cow price), national milk production, annual milk yield per cow, number of dairy cows, calving interval, cow replacement rate
- Estimates of disease impacts on milk yield, fertility, and culling
- Regional estimates of incidence or prevalence of dairy cattle diseases

Selected results are displayed in the following table, presenting the annual losses and average losses per cow across diseases in dairy cattle (mean values and standard deviation in parenthesis) in North America (adapted from Tables 6 and 7 of the published article [3]. North American results were selected for comparability with the cost of disease study.

Disease	Total annual losses (USD, in billions)	Average annual losses per cow (USD)
Clinical ketosis	0.02 (0.01)	1.18 (1.09)
Clinical mastitis	2.02 (0.16)	153.99 (12.41)
Displaced abomasum	0.06 (0.03)	4.56 (2.14)
Dystocia	0.13 (0.04)	10.05 (3.17)
Lameness	0.81 (0.10)	61.64 (7.85)
Metritis	0.77 (0.10)	58.53 (7.65)
Milk fever	0.06 (0.03)	4.33 (2.08)
Ovarian cyst	0.73 (0.10)	55.76 (7.47)
Paratuberculosis	0.58 (0.09)	44.16 (6.65)
Retained placenta	0.47 (0.08)	35.89 (5.99)
Subclinical ketosis	2.84 (0.19)	216.17 (14.7)
Subclinical mastitis	1.57 (0.14)	119.38 (10.93)
Total	**10.07 (0.5)**	**765.64 (38.00)**

▶ Important Note:
The losses per cow were calculated, considering prevalence or incidence of the diseases. Thus, they represent the average losses spread over all cows, not the loss experienced by an affected animal.

Maybe you have noted from the input data listed in Box 7.1 that this study did not consider treatment cost. So, how can we compare results of this study with those estimated in the cost of disease study, which actually included treatment costs?

An approach is presented in Box 7.2.

Box 7.2 Cost of Dairy Diseases Versus Burden of Dairy Diseases

The problem: the cost of disease study [2] considered treatment costs, whereas the burden of disease study did not [3]. In the following you will find a potential approach to allow a comparison of results:

- To make the results of the two studies comparable, we adjusted the per-cow losses reported in the burden of disease study by the share of veterinary and treatment costs reported in the cost of disease study:

	Cost of disease study [2]					Burden of disease study [3]		
Disease	Parity	Total costs (USD)	Vet/treatment costs (USD)	Costs without vet/treatment (USD)	% of vet/treatment costs from costs without vet/treatment	Average cost per cow (USD)	Average Vet/Treatment costs (USD)	Adjusted average costs per cow (USD)
Mastitis	Primiparous	325.76	77.74	248.02	31%	153.99	153.99 × 0.31 = 47.74	153.99 + 47.74 = **201.73**
	Multiparous	426.50	77.74	348.76	22%			
Displaced Abomasum	Primiparous	432.48	197.22	235.26	84%	4.56	4.56 × 0.84 = 3.83	4.56 + 3.83 = **8.39**
	Multiparous	639.51	197.22	442.29	45%			

Conclusions:

- Clinical mastitis remains roughly 24 times costlier per cow than displaced abomasum
- Even applying the higher percentages, as calculated in primiparous cows, the cost assumptions cannot bring displaced abomasum anywhere near the top three diseases in the USA as estimated in the burden of disease study, because prevalence and incidence of displaced abomasum is much lower than that of clinical mastitis

7.1.3 Global Burden of Animal Diseases

The Global Burden of Animal Diseases (GBADs) program was launched in 2018 [4], being inspired by the success of the Global Burden of Disease (GBD) study in human health. For more information on the human health project, we refer to Box 7.3, which provides a brief overview.

The GBADs is a landmark international initiative designed to systematically assess the economic, social, and environmental impacts of animal diseases and related interventions. The program was conceived in response to the growing recognition of the impact that animal diseases have on global health, food security, livelihoods, and economies, particularly in low- and middle-income countries where livestock are integral to livelihoods, nutrition, and economic resilience. The aim of the program is to quantify the burden animal diseases place on society and guide resources toward improvements in animal health leading to more efficient and sustainable production and food systems. Thereby, the program incorporates One Health principles, emphasizing the interconnectedness of animal, human, and environmental health. All information obtained is intended to be made available to smallholders and farmers, businesses, governments, and wider society as a global public good.

Within the program, standardized metrics and tools have been developed to evaluate the burden of diseases in livestock, poultry, aquaculture, and companion animals. An example of such a tool has been briefly described in the last section (Sect. 7.1.2), the comorbidity adjustment [3].

Box 7.3 Global Burden of Disease Study

The Global Burden of Disease study is coordinated by the Institute for Health Metrics and Evaluation (IHME) [6] and represents one of the most comprehensive health research initiatives globally. It publishes a wide array of health data and metrics designed to assess the overall impact of diseases, injuries, and risk factors across countries, age groups, and over time. Among others, it has led to the development of the disability-adjusted life year (DALY), a groundbreaking advancement in global health metrics, enabling policymakers to systematically compare and prioritize disease burdens across populations and time.

▶ Short Note:
The DALY combines years of life lost due to premature death with years lived with disability, allowing burden of disease studies to capture both mortality and morbidity. It will be explained in detail in Chap. 14 of this book, which is entirely dedicated to this measure, thereby also presenting first studies that have adapted the DALY for use in animal health.

In the same context, Gilbert et al. (2024) developed a new metric, the Animal Health Loss Envelope (AHLE). The tool shows the total financial costs of an animal disease at farm level. It sums the value of production lost because animals perform below their disease-free potential and the expenditures for disease control, and compares this to a disease-free ideal. The authors gave a practical example of the calculations, a model of intensive poultry production aimed at rearing broiler chickens [5].

7.2 Eradication Programs

Eradication programs represent the most ambitious type of disease control effort as they aim to eliminate a disease entirely from the global population. These initiatives are rare, costly, and long-term, and need thorough assessments of the burden of diseases to justify the effort. At the time of this writing, only one animal disease (rinderpest) has been officially eradicated in 2011. The eradication was achieved through the Global Rinderpest Eradication Program, a joint Food and Agriculture Organization (FAO) and World Organization for Animal Health (OIE) effort. The United Nations approximated that the total costs of rinderpest eradication from 1945 to 2011 was USD 5 billion [7].

Following this precedent, a new eradication target was announced in 2015: peste des petits ruminants (PPR). Often referred to as "goat plague," PPR poses a major threat to small ruminant populations and the livelihoods of millions of rural families. The goal is to eradicate PPR by 2030. Financial modeling estimated that the global 15-year campaign would cost undiscounted between USD 7.6 and 9.1 billion, with USD 2.5 to 3.1 billion needed for the first 5 years [8].

Such figures underscore the importance of economic evaluations in eradication planning. They help decision-makers prioritize diseases and allocate funding efficiently, especially in a world with limited resources and competing health challenges.

Although eradication campaigns are costly upfront, they offer long-term, lasting benefits. They eliminate the need for repeated treatments or vaccinations, they help prevent cross-border reintroductions, strengthen the resilience of food systems and communities, and ultimately improve animal welfare over time.

Take-Home Messages

- Cost of disease studies estimate the economic impact of a health disorder, either on a per-case basis or across populations.
- Burden of disease studies quantify the total impact of a disease on animal populations by combining its frequency (prevalence or incidence) with the severity of outcomes, i.e., economic, health-related, and sometimes social or environmental aspects, at farm, regional, national, or global level.
- A disease with the highest cost per case may not represent the greatest burden if it occurs infrequently.

- The Global Burden of Animal Diseases (GBADs) program aims to deliver comprehensive, standardized assessments of the economic, social, and environmental impacts of animal diseases, with a particular focus on low- and middle-income countries.
- Understanding the costs of eradication or control programs is essential for prioritizing diseases and supporting evidence-based investment decisions.

References

1. Oxford Analytica (2012) The Costs of Animal Disease. International Federation for Animal Health. https://healthforanimals.org/resources/publications/publications/white-paper-the-costs-of-animal-disease/. Assessed 04 May 2025
2. Liang D, Arnold LM, Stowe CJ, Harmon RJ, Bewley JM (2017) Estimating US dairy clinical disease costs with a stochastic simulation model. J Dairy Sci 100:1472–1486
3. Rasmussen P, Barkema HW, Osei PP, Taylor J, Shaw AP, Conrady B et al (2024) Global losses due to dairy cattle diseases: a comorbidity-adjusted economic analysis. J Dairy Sci 107:6945–6970
4. Rushton J, Bruce M, Bellet C, Torgerson P, Shaw A, Marsh T et al (2018) Initiation of global burden of animal diseases Programme. Lancet 392:538–540
5. Gilbert W, Marsh TL, Chaters G, Jemberu WT, Bruce M, Steeneveld W et al (2024) Quantifying cost of disease in livestock: a new metric for the Global Burden of Animal Diseases. Lancet Planet Health 8:e309
6. Institute for Health Metrics and Evaluation. https://www.healthdata.org/research-analysis/gbd. Assessed: 04 May 2025
7. Youde J (2013) Cattle scourge no more: the eradication of rinderpest and its lessons for global health campaigns. Politics Life Sci 32(1):43–57
8. Food and Agriculture Organization of the United Nations, World Organisation for Animal Health 2015) Global control and eradication of peste des petits ruminants. https://wwwwo-ahorg/app/uploads/2021/03/ppr-advocacy-enpdf Assessed: 04 May 2025

Cost-Minimization Analysis 8

Abstract

A cost-minimization analysis (CMA) compares two or more health interventions, focusing exclusively on costs. This type of study is only applicable when the health interventions of interest have equal effectiveness. However, this is rare in human and veterinary medicine. Treatments proven equally effective in randomized controlled trials conducted for licensing may differ in effectiveness, when used in broader animal populations. Even generic drugs can differ in their pharmacokinetics in specific situations. When using human generic drugs in pets, pharmacokinetics can differ, because bioequivalence in humans does not always equate to bioequivalence in animals due to differences in gastrointestinal tract anatomy and physiology. In countries with less stringent quality control for approval of veterinary pharmaceuticals, generic drugs can broadly differ in pharmacokinetics from the original patented drug. Nonetheless, we present an example, comparing the costs of different treatments for African animal trypanosomiasis in Uganda. In most African countries, veterinary services have been decentralized and privatized and livestock keepers bear the costs of most services. In such settings, where interventions must fit limited budgets, CMA might be a pragmatic approach.

Keywords
Cost-minimization analysis · Generic drugs · Pharmacokinetics

B. Poulsen Nautrup, *Outcomes Research in Animal Health Care*,
https://doi.org/10.1007/978-3-032-12587-3_8

8.1 Definition and Application

As the name cost-minimization analysis (CMA) suggests, this comparative analysis focuses exclusively on costs and is only appropriate when the health interventions of interest have the same effectiveness. However, such a scenario is rare in both human and veterinary medicine. In most cases, not only costs but also effectiveness differs between interventions, making cost-benefit or cost-effectiveness analyses the appropriate type of study, which allow the consideration of both, costs and effectiveness. These analyses are described in detail in the following Chaps. 9 and 10.

But why are there only few instances, in which a CMA would be indicated? The following examples will give an answer:

- Drugs with different ingredients are rarely equally effective. However, two different drugs sometimes show the same outcome in randomized comparative trials (RCTs). This is often the case if the company uses an equivalence trial or non-inferiority trial during the developmental phase, intended to show that a new drug is equal or not worse than an established one. In this case, a CMA may be reasonable, if results indicate clinical equivalence. However, once the new drug is used in a broader population of animals, real-world outcomes might shift. For example, acceptance or ease-of application may differ if the drugs have different application forms. Or very rare adverse events might only become evident after widespread use. Both factors can significantly impact the outcome, and the drugs can no longer be regarded as equally effective. Accordingly, even if a CMA may be an appropriate tool initially, it should be reconsidered if subsequent evidence reveals important differences undetected in the limited setting of an RCT. (We refer to Chap. 3 for detailed information on the difference between efficacy, as measured in controlled trials, and effectiveness, observed in daily practice.)
- Generic drugs can also lead to different outcomes in daily practice. Again, the compliance may differ between two drugs with identical active ingredients, but different application formulations. In specific situations, generic drugs have also been shown to differ in pharmacokinetic properties. In Box 8.1 we have included two examples of varying pharmacokinetics between generic drugs.

In conclusion, two different drugs or health interventions seldom produce identical outcomes under real-world conditions, thus limiting the use of CMA. As early as 2001, Briggs and O'Brian hypothesized "the death of cost-minimization analysis" in human health economics [1].

Box 8.1 Examples of Variations in Pharmacokinetics Among Generic Drugs
We have collected two examples from different veterinary areas to illustrate situations, in which pharmacokinetics have been shown to differ between generic drugs.

1. *A generic antifungal drug in dogs and cats*
   A study investigated the clinical pharmacokinetics of human-approved generic fluconazole in client-owned dogs and cats with fungal disease. Random inter-animal pharmacokinetic variability was high in both species. Two dogs experienced nearly two-fold increases in serum fluconazole when generic formulations were changed, suggesting a lack of bioequivalence. The authors concluded that bioequivalence in humans does not necessarily translate to bioequivalence in animals due to differences in gastrointestinal tract anatomy and physiology [2].
2. *A generic antiparasitic drug in heifers*
   Triclabendazole has been extensively used to treat fasciolosis in sheep and cattle. A study compared the pharmacokinetics of the originally patented drug with four generics available in Peru. Only one generic drug was deemed equivalent to the original. The authors emphasized the need for stricter quality control in veterinary drug approval in some regions of the world [3].

▶ Conclusions:
Even with generic drug formulations, differences in bioavailability can significantly impact effectiveness.

8.2 Example of Cost-Minimization Analysis

Despite the above-mentioned limitations, CMAs may be appropriate in certain circumstances. A study comparing the costs of different programs targeting African animal trypanosomiasis in Uganda represents a practical use of CMA in veterinary medicine. The study estimated the costs of different methods to control the cattle disease in rural Uganda, calculating all related expenses, including equipment, labor, and community efforts, to see which methods were most affordable for small farmers. In most African countries, including Uganda, veterinary services have been decentralized and privatized, and livestock keepers bear the costs of most services. Consequently, treatments and other health care interventions must fit their budgets to be feasible [4]. While not ideal, restricting an economic analysis to costs might be a pragmatic decision in low-resource settings, where budget pressure outweights differences in efficacy.

Take-Home Messages

- Cost-minimization analysis (CMA) focuses exclusively on costs and is applicable only when two health interventions have equal effectiveness, which is a rare situation in veterinary medicine.
- Treatments proven equally effective in randomized controlled trials conducted for licensing may also differ in effectiveness, when used in broader animal populations and daily practice.
- Even generic drugs can lead to different outcomes in real-world setting, and equal effectiveness cannot always be assumed.
- However, in low-resource settings, where interventions must fit limited budgets, CMA might be a pragmatic approach.

References

1. Briggs AH, O'Brien BJ (2001) The death of cost-minimization analysis? Health Econ 10:179–184
2. KuKanich K, KuKanich B, Lin Z, Rankin AJ, Hanzlicek AS, Palerme J-S et al (2020) Clinical pharmacokinetics and outcomes of oral fluconazole therapy in dogs and cats with naturally occurring fungal disease. J Vet Pharmacol Ther 43:547–556
3. Ortiz P, Castope N, Cabrera M, Farias C, Suarez G, Lanusse C et al (2014) Pharmacokinetic evaluation of different generic triclabendazole formulations in heifers. N Z Vet J 62(5):279–285
4. Muhanguzi D, Okello WO, Kabasa JD, Waiswa C, Welburn SC, Shaw APM (2015) Cost analysis of options for management of African Animal Trypanosomiasis using interventions targeted at cattle in Tororo District; South-Eastern Uganda. Parasit Vectors 8:387

9 Cost-Benefit Analysis & Partial Budget Analysis

Abstract

In cost-benefit analyses (CBAs) and partial budget analysis, all parameters, i.e., costs and effects, are expressed in monetary units. These approaches are the common types of health economic analysis in the livestock sector. Social CBAs are used to guide decisions on large-scale programs with broad societal significance, such as national or global disease control initiatives. Private CBAs assess whether a livestock venture is economically viable by comparing the cost of a health or management intervention with the benefits, typically measured in terms of increased productivity. Partial budgeting, on the other hand, is the preferred method to evaluate the economic impact of relatively small management changes. It considers only those costs and benefits that are directly affected by the intervention. The outcomes of CBAs are commonly expressed as net present value (the present difference between benefits and costs), benefit-cost ratio (the ratio of net present benefits and net present costs) or internal rate of return (the discount rate that makes the net present value zero). Results from partial budgeting are mainly expressed as change of profit due to an intervention. Unlike partial budget analyses, CBAs often span several years, and therefore require discounting to account for the time value of money.

Keywords

Cost-benefit analysis · Partial budgeting · Delta profit · Net present value · Benefit-cost ratio · Internal rate of return · Discounting · Externalities

9.1 Introductory Remarks

Cost-benefit analysis (CBA) and partial budgeting (partial budget analysis) are economic tools commonly used in animal health care to evaluate the net economic benefit of health or management interventions. Both concepts aim to assess whether

B. Poulsen Nautrup, *Outcomes Research in Animal Health Care*,
https://doi.org/10.1007/978-3-032-12587-3_9

an intervention is economically justifiable, serving as key instruments for rational resource allocation. Since all parameters, costs and effects, are expressed in monetary units, these tools have traditionally been applied in livestock management, where health benefits can be readily quantified. Livestock animals typically have a defined market value, and health impairments can be expressed as losses due to decreased productivity. For example, in dairy cows, pain may lead to a decline in milk yield which can be quantified, and the economic benefit of treatment is expressed as the avoided loss in milk production.

In contrast, outcomes in companion animals are often more difficult to express in monetary terms. For instance, relieving a pet's pain obviously improves its quality of life. But how to express this improvement in monetary units? And in the event of a pet's death, the emotional value to the owner may far exceed the replacement costs. Although the willingness-to-pay approach can assist in translating health impairments in pets into monetary values, CBAs and partial budgeting remain predominantly applied in the livestock sector.

▶ Short Note on "Willingness-to-Pay"
The willingness-to-pay approach in animal health care is a method used to assess the monetary value that animal owners or stakeholders assign to veterinary services, treatments, or health outcomes in animals. It reflects how much people are willing to pay for a specific intervention, representing the perceived value of the health impairment caused by the intervention.

9.2 Key Features of CBA & Partial Budgeting

This section begins with a summary table that outlines the main features of CBA and partial budgeting, providing a clear overview of their respective characteristics and key differences.

It is important to distinguish not only between CBA and partial budgeting but also between social and private CBAs. Social CBAs are designed to inform decisions on large-scale initiatives with broad societal relevance, such as national or global disease control programs. Private CBAs assess if a specific intervention is economically viable by comparing its costs with the benefits gained through higher productivity and less losses, helping stakeholders such as farmers optimize their investment decisions. Partial budgeting, on the other hand, is typically used to evaluate the economic impact of small management changes by focusing exclusively on the costs and benefits directly affected by the intervention.

Accordingly, the three approaches primarily differ in their scope, which narrows progressively from social CBA, to private CBA, to partial budgeting. Table 9.1 provides an overview of the main characteristics of each type of analysis, which are further illustrated with practical examples in Sect. 9.5.

Table 9.1 Differences between social and private CBA and partial budget analysis

Aspect	Social CBA	Private CBA	Partial budgeting
Perspective	Society as a whole	Individual, business, or private entity	Farm or business level, focusing on a specific change
Scope	Broad (includes all societal, environmental, and economic impacts)	Narrower (focuses on private profits and costs)	Very narrow (focuses on marginal changes in a specific scenario)
Costs included	Private and external costs (e.g., pollution, human health impacts)	Only private costs (e.g., inputs, labor, capital)	Only costs that change due to the proposed intervention
Benefits included	Private and external benefits (e.g., externalities)	Typically, only private benefits	Only benefits that change as a result of the intervention
Decision focus	Social welfare and optimal resource allocation	Individual profit maximization	Economic feasibility of a specific intervention
Time Horizon	Often long-term	Short-to-medium term (often considering more than 1 year)	Short term (often not exceeding 1 year)
Discounting	Yes	If time horizon is >1 year: yes	If time horizon is <1 year: no
Common results	Net present value, benefit-cost ratio, internal rate of return	Net present value, benefit-cost ratio, internal rate of return	Change in profit
Complexity	High	Moderate	Low (quick and simple comparison)
Common Use	Disease control programs, One Health	Investment decisions, project planning	Farm management decisions, minor operational changes

9.3 Reporting Results

Results of CBA are commonly expressed as net present value, benefit-cost ratio, or internal rate of return [1].

▶ Important Note:
If the CBA exceeds one year, net present benefit corresponds to the present value of all future benefit cash-flows, and net present cost corresponds to the present value of all future cost cash flows, i.e., both items need to be discounted. (More information on discounting is included in Sect. 9.4.1)

- *Net present value (NPV)* is the simple mathematical difference between the present value of an intervention's monetary benefits and its costs. The corresponding formula is

$$net\ present\ benefit - net\ present\ cost = net\ present\ value$$

When the NPV is above zero, the program's return is higher than the opportunity cost of the invested money.

- *Benefit-cost ratio (BCR)* is calculated by dividing the present value of benefit by the present value of cost, thus describing the relative size of the two parameters. The formula is

$$\frac{net\ present\ benefit}{net\ present\ cost} = benefit - cost\ ratio$$

  If the BCR is greater than 1, the returns exceed the costs. In that case, the NPV must be greater than zero.
- *Internal rate of return (IRR)* is less intuitive, but useful for allocating investments. The IRR is defined as the interest rate that reduces the NPV to zero. If the IRR exceeds the interest rate, one could earn with alternative uses of the money, the investment is economically attractive. Commonly, financial software tools, such as a built-in function in MS Excel™, are used to determine the IRR, as it involves iterative calculations.

Results from partial budget analysis are commonly reported as change in profit, also called Delta profit (Δ-profit) or net benefit change.

- *Delta profit or net benefit change*, represents the change in profit. Only the expenses and income that would be altered by the management change are entered into a partial budget, and the Δ-profit is calculated, considering the following four components:

$$Increased\ revenues + decreased\ costs - increased\ costs - decreased\ revenues = \Delta - profit$$

▶ Short Note:
Although at first glance, NPV and Δ-profit may appear similar, there is a key distinction between the two: Δ-profit is the simple difference between profits before and after an intervention, without accounting for the timing of cash flows. In contrast, NPV captures the value of all future cash flows associated with an intervention, discounted back to their present value. Accordingly, if the partial budget horizon exceeds 1 year, discounting should be applied and the resulting discounted Δ-profit will numerically equal the NPV. Nevertheless, the two measures are often used for different purposes: NPV is typically applied to provide a comprehensive, long-term economic assessment, while Δ-profit is more commonly used for comparing short-term scenarios or management changes.

9.4 Key Aspects of CBA

There are two important aspects of CBA that warrant special attention: discounting and externalities.

9.4.1 Why Do We Need Discounting?

Often part of the costs and benefits of health care programs in livestock arise in the future rather than being confined to the first year. As a result, both social and private

CBAs typically span more than 1 year and therefore require discounting of future costs and benefits. The rationale for discounting lies in the principle that money available today is generally considered more valuable than the same amount in the future, due to its potential to earn interest or to be invested elsewhere. Chapter 6 provides a more detailed explanation of the concept of discounting and the methods used for calculation. While discounting is essential for multiyear projects, the discount rate may vary over time and between countries.

In contrast, partial budget analysis generally applies to short-term scenarios, which cover typically less than 1 year, where discounting is not necessary.

9.4.2 What Are Externalities?

An important aspect of social CBA is the consideration of externalities. Externalities are unintended side effects of interventions that affect individuals or groups beyond those directly involved. These externalities can be either positive or negative and are especially relevant in animal health, where the impacts of interventions often extend beyond the farm level.

- *Positive externalities* occur when an intervention produces broader societal benefits. For example, vaccinating livestock against zoonotic diseases, such as brucellosis, not only protects the animals but also reduces the risk of transmission to humans, thereby enhancing public health. Similarly, controlling infectious diseases within a single herd can lower the likelihood of spread to neighboring farms, contributing to the health and stability of the wider agricultural community.
- *Negative Externalities*, on the other hand, arise when the broader consequences of an intervention are harmful. For instance, an overuse of antibiotics in animals can contribute to the development of antimicrobial resistance, which poses a global health risk to both humans and animals. Another example is the improper disposal of animal waste, which can lead to environmental contamination, adversely affecting water quality, ecosystems, and public health beyond the boundaries of the originating farm.

9.5 Practical Examples

9.5.1 What Characterizes Social CBAs?

Social CBAs adopt a broad perspective by evaluating the wider societal impact of animal health interventions. Unlike private analyses that focus on individual economic outcomes, social CBAs consider how an intervention affects public health, environmental sustainability, and overall social welfare. These analyses are essential for informing decisions about large-scale health initiatives, such as national or international disease control programs, where the benefits and costs extend beyond individual stakeholders. Before allocating funding for such programs, a social CBA should be conducted to assess the projected societal benefits relative to the required investment. The example presented in Box 9.1 illustrates this approach by evaluating the impact of a mass vaccination campaign in Mongolia.

Box 9.1 Social Cost-Benefit Analysis of Mass Vaccination in Mongolia

Roth et al. (2003) published a study investigating the impact of mass vaccination of ruminants against the zoonotic disease brucellosis [2]. Brucellosis is a bacterial disease leading to reduced reproduction and fertility, reduced survival of newborns, and reduced milk yield in affected animals. Humans become infected by exposure to infected livestock and livestock products, showing extreme weakness, joint and muscle pain, headache, undulant fever, and sweating, that can continue for several years.
(Only parts of the study will be presented here for illustrative purposes.)

Methods: The cost-benefit analysis considered

- *Intervention*: 10-year national vaccination program targeting cattle and small ruminants
- *Protection scenario*: 52% reduction in transmission
- *Discount rate*: 5%
- *Costs considered*:
  - Agriculture sector: vaccine, delivery, logistics, diagnostics, ear tags, surveillance, and training
  - Health sector: costs of human brucellosis (Ministry-of-Health costs, patient's out-of-pocket expenses, income losses)
- *Benefits considered*:
  - Agriculture sector: avoidance of losses in animals and animal products
  - Health sector: avoidance of human cases and their economic consequences

Results (adapted from Table 2 of [2]): Costs in million USD, converted from MNT, using the conversion rate as of 2000)

Sector	Costs	Benefits	Net present value	Benefit-cost ratio
Agriculture	4.8	15.4	10.6	3.2
Human health	3.5	11.2	7.7	3.2
Total society	8.3	26.6	18.3	3.2

Conclusions: The program yields more than three dollars of benefit for every dollar invested.

▶ Important Note:
The study also considered intangible effects of human brucellosis, using the disability-adjusted life year (DALY), a measure of healthy life years lost, combining the years of life lost from premature mortality with the years lived with disability, weighted by a disease-specific severity factor. The DALY concept will be explained and discussed in detail in Chap. 14, also describing first adaptations to animal health care.

9.5.2 What Are Private CBAs Used For?

Private cost–benefit analysis (CBA) evaluates the economic feasibility of a health or management intervention from the perspective of an individual stakeholder, such as a farmer, herd manager, or company. The purpose is to assess whether an investment in treatment, prevention, or management practice is likely to generate a positive return, either through increased productivity or reduced costs. Box 9.2 provides an illustrative example of a private CBA, examining a program designed to reduce the prevalence of paratuberculosis in a cattle herd.

Box 9.2 Example of a Private CBA, Considering Discounting of Costs and Benefits

Marsh (1999) published a fictive, albeit illustrative example of a private CBA, investigating a program to reduce the prevalence of paratuberculosis in a cattle herd over a five-year planning horizon, thereby also considering the discounting of future costs and benefits [1].

Methods: The CBA considered

- Costs of program,
- Benefits of the reduced incidence of paratuberculosis, which were cexpected after year 1 onwards
- Discount rate for costs and benefits: 5% (i.e., 0.05)

Results (adapted from Table II of [1]):

Year	Costs	Benefits	Discounted costs	Discounted benefits	Discounted cash flows
0	15,000	0	15,000	0	−15,000
1	10,000	4500	9524	4286	–5238
2	1500	15,000	1361	13,605	12,245
3	1000	13,000	864	11,230	10,366
4	5000	8000	4114	6582	2468
5	0	5000	0	3918	3918
Total	32,500	45,500	30,863	39,621	8759

Calculations:

- Discounting year 1
  - Costs: USD 10,000/(1 + 0.05) = USD 9524
  - Benefits: USD 4500/(1 + 0.05) = USD 4286 USD
  - Cash flow: USD 4285 – USD 9524 = USD – 5238

  The calculations for the following years follow the same approach.
- Outcomes
  - NPV: USD 39,621 – USD 30,863 = USD 8759
  - BCR: USD 39,621/USD 30,863 = 1.28
  - IRR: = 20.46% (calculated with computer software)

(Small discrepancies in the calculations are due to rounding)

▶ Short Note:
The table includes another useful calculation, the discounted cash flow that shows which years yield losses and which produce returns above costs.

9.5.3 What Makes Partial Budget Analysis Different?

The partial budget analysis is a simple economic tool used to assess the financial impact of a specific change in farm management, such as adopting a new disease control option, without requiring a full financial analysis of the entire operation. In animal health, this analysis is particularly useful for evaluating the costs and benefits of interventions like vaccinations, changes in housing, or biosecurity measures. Only the expenses and income that would be altered by the change are entered into a partial budget. It is a practical first-step analysis that helps farmers and advisors decide whether a proposed health or management intervention is likely to be economically worthwhile. An example of a partial budget analysis is provided in Box 9.3.

9.6 Common Drawbacks of CBAs & Partial Budgeting

The three described analyses have been criticized for their limited consideration of animal welfare. For instance, while treating a dairy cow in pain may lead to improved productivity, it also enhances the animal's well-being, an important outcome that traditional CBA and partial budgeting often fail to capture. Although recent methodological developments have sought to incorporate welfare metrics into economic evaluations of livestock interventions, these approaches remain relatively uncommon. In the final part of this book (Part IV), we will introduce some of these emerging methods, with a focus on how animal quality of life and welfare can be integrated into health economic frameworks.

In terms of technical complexity, private CBAs and partial budgeting can often be carried out using straightforward spreadsheet tools. In contrast, social CBAs generally require more advanced analytical techniques and are associated with more demanding data requirements. Moreover, the outcomes of social CBAs can be sensitive even to small changes in key input parameters. This issue can be addressed through sensitivity analysis, which systematically explores how variations in factors such as discount rates, costs, and productivity affect the results. The principles and application of sensitivity analysis will be discussed in detail and illustrated in Chap. 11.

Take-Home Messages

- In cost-benefit analyses (CBAs) and partial budgeting, all parameters, both costs and effects, are expressed in monetary terms, making these methods the most commonly used economic evaluation tools in livestock.
- Social CBAs support decision-making for large-scale programs with broad societal relevance, such as national or global disease control initiatives.
- Private CBAs evaluate the economic viability of livestock interventions by comparing their costs with the anticipated productivity gains, typically over a multi-year period.
- Partial budgeting is best suited for assessing the economic impact of small-scale management changes, focusing exclusively on the costs and benefits directly affected by the intervention.

Box 9.3 Partial Budget Analysis

Jerlström et al. (2022) applied a partial budget analysis to assess the economic impact of avoiding the mixing of litters after weaning in a 355-sow Swedish farrow-to-finish pig farm (strategy S1). This intervention aimed to reduce the prevalence of lung lesions at slaughter, which indicate respiratory disease with impaired productivity and economic losses that had occurred during the animal's lifetime. In-put data were derived from official databases, publications, and expert opinion. (Although the authors evaluated two different strategies, we focus here only on the first one) [3].

Results (adapted from Table 6 of [3]):

Benefit change (SEK) (Positive Cash-Flow Items)		Cost change (SEK) (Negative Cash-Flow Items)	
Increased revenues		*Decreased revenues*	
No new revenues	0	Decreased carcass sales due to sub-optimal use of space (foregone pigs)	196,295
Decreased costs		*Increased costs*	
Decreased costs of medicine, treatment, and vet visits	3693	Increased feed costs for healthier pigs	58,050
Decreased labor hours at finishing stage	59,826	Increased labor input for pigs	2001
Decreased cost of daily feed for foregone pigs	157,317	Increased labor hours at weaning	2005
Decreased cost of carcass disposal	44,994		
Decreased deduction costs for lung lesions at meat inspection	26,106		
Subtotal	*291,936*	*Subtotal*	*258,351*
Net (benefit) change (Δ-profit)			*+ 33,585*

Conclusions: In this example, avoiding mixing of litters after weaning leads to an increased annual net income of SEK 33,585 or EUR 3123 (exchange rate as valid at the time of analysis).

▶ Important Note:

For the sake of simplicity, the results presented here are based on a deterministic analysis, which uses fixed values for each input parameter. However, the authors also conducted simulations, in which input parameters were represented by probability distributions rather than single point estimates. This approach accounts for variability and uncertainty in the data and corresponds to a probabilistic sensitivity analysis, which is discussed in greater detail in Chap. 11.

References

1. Marsh W (1999) The economics of animal health in farmed livestock at the herd level. Rev Sci Tech Off Int Epiz 18(2):357–366
2. Roth F, Zinsstag J, Orkhon D, Chimed-Ochir G, Hutton G, Cosivi O et al (2003) Human health benefits from livestock vaccination for brucellosis: case study. Bull World Health Organ 81(12):867–876
3. Jerlström J, Huang W, Ehlorsson C-J, Eriksson I, Reneby A, Comin A (2022) Stochastic partial budget analysis of strategies to reduce the prevalence of lung lesions in finishing pigs at slaughter. Front Vet Sci 9:957975

Cost-Effectiveness Analysis 10

Abstract

Cost-effectiveness analysis (CEA) is a systematic method of comparing two or more alternative interventions by calculating their costs and health outcomes, ultimately expressing costs in relation to their effectiveness. Because the health outcomes, such as life years gained or improvements in animal welfare, remain in their natural units rather than being monetized, CEA is well suited to decision-making across all animal health settings, including companion animals. Results are often expressed as incremental cost-effectiveness ratio, such as the cost per additional life year gained with a new therapy compared to current standard treatment. CEA often uses decision trees and Markov models to simulate outcomes over time. Both models allow the consideration of data and information from many sources and can model the outcomes over a longer time period as considered in clinical studies A decision tree is much simpler than a Markov model, but it is an intuitive tool to display simple disease and treatment processes. A Markov model is especially useful for approximating long-term outcomes when animals progress through different health states, e.g., progress over time through states of varying severity.

Keywords

Cost-effectiveness analysis · Incremental cost-effectiveness ratio · ICER · Decision tree · Markov model · Cost-effectiveness plane · Bubble diagram

10.1 The Significance of Cost-Effectiveness Analysis

A cost-effectiveness analysis (CEA) is a systematic method of comparing two or more alternative interventions or programs by calculating their costs and health outcomes, ultimately expressing costs in relation to their effectiveness. This approach

B. Poulsen Nautrup, *Outcomes Research in Animal Health Care*,
https://doi.org/10.1007/978-3-032-12587-3_10

avoids expressing health effects such as life years gained or improvement in quality of life or animal welfare in monetary units. For this reason, CEA has become the predominant analysis in human health care. There are also various applications for CEA in animal health care:

- CEAs can help governments and organizations make informed decisions about disease control and prevention programs. And many CEAs in the field of animal health analyze programs focusing on the control of *zoonotic diseases* [1]. In case of zoonosis, outcomes are typically expressed as the cost per human death averted or the cost per disability-adjusted life year (DALY) averted. A DALY is a combined measure of life years lost due to disability and premature mortality that will be discussed in detail in Chap. 14.
- In *livestock*, diseases often lead to production losses, such as reduced growth or lower milk yield, that can be quantified in monetary terms. For this reason, cost-benefit analyses (which are the topic of Chap. 9) remain the dominant analysis in these animals [2]. However, CEAs are useful when evaluating the effect of interventions in livestock on the environment such as greenhouse gas emissions, with results being expressed as cost per ton of reduced emissions of CO_2 equivalents [3]. Additionally, animal welfare is becoming more important in livestock, being increasingly considered as decision point beside economics [4]. Therefore, in future CEAs may play a more important role also in farm animals.
- In the field of *companion animals*, CEAs have already been conducted and published, and two of them will serve as examples in the next sections of this chapter. Because health outcomes are expressed in natural units, such as life years gained, rather being converted into monetary values, CEAs are particularly well suited to analyses in the companion animal context. Nevertheless, they have yet to achieve the same level of popularity as in human health care.

To promote broader adoption, the Food and Agriculture Organization (FAO) of the United Nations has published an "*Introduction to the Use of Cost-Effectiveness Analysis in Animal Health,*" which advocates for the wider application of CEAs in veterinary contexts [1]. Supporting this perspective, researchers from the Royal Veterinary College in the UK have emphasized: "As in human health, it is likely that CEA will become increasingly predominant in assessments of animal health, production, and welfare, emphasizing the importance of understanding the strength and limitations of this tool" [2].

10.2 The Basic Concept of CEA

10.2.1 The Ultimate Outcome: Incremental Cost-Effectiveness Ratio (ICER)

As mentioned earlier, CEAs compare the costs of two or more alternative interventions in relation to their health outcomes. To ensure valid comparisons, all alternatives must be measured in the same unit, which should represent a health effect of relevance for the patient rather than surrogate parameters. In dogs, published examples of such relevant outcomes include the time without symptoms of disease [5] or the number of additional life days gained [6]. The latter study expressed the final results as cost per additional life day gained. This outcome is also called incremental cost-effectiveness ratio (ICER). The ICER expresses the additional cost required to gain one extra unit of health benefit, such as one more life day gained.

But how to calculate the ICER? CEAs follow an incremental approach by comparing two or more interventions: they calculate the difference in total costs (incremental costs) and the difference in health outcomes (incremental effectiveness) between the alternative options. The ICER is then derived by dividing the incremental costs by the incremental effectiveness. While this may appear rather complex at first glance, the example in Box 10.1 will help clarify the calculations.

In our simplified example, the new therapy is more expensive but also more effective, a common scenario in CEAs. However, a new therapy may be cost-saving and more effective than the comparator; in that case, it is considered the dominant strategy. This may seem unlikely, as new drugs, for example, are often more expensive than old (generic) drugs. But if a new drug, for instance, reduces the incidence of complications which require additional (expensive) treatments, total cost of care may actually be lower than with current therapy (a good reminder of the importance to consider total costs of therapy, not only the upfront costs of a drug or intervention).

Box 10.1 Simplified Example of CEA

In this fictive and simplified example, total costs and average life expectancy have been estimated for two treatments (the new and current one) of a severe disease in cats:

Total costs of new treatment:	USD 242.50
Total costs of current treatment:	USD 172.50
Incremental costs:	**USD 70.00**
Life expectancy with new therapy:	3.83 years
Life expectancy with current therapy:	3.15 years
Incremental effectiveness:	**0.68 years**

The incremental cost effectiveness ratio is calculated by dividing the incremental costs by incremental effectiveness:

ICER: 70.00 USD/0.68 years = *102.94 USD per additional life year gained with the new therapy*

10.2.2 A Useful Tool: The Cost-Effectiveness Plane

To better understand the results of a cost-effectiveness analysis (CEA), we can visualize them using a two-dimensional graph called the cost-effectiveness plane. In this graph:

- The x-axis shows the difference in effectiveness between two interventions.
- The y-axis shows the difference in their costs.

The comparator, often the current or standard therapy, is placed at the origin (0,0). Each alternative therapy can then be positioned on the plane based on how much more or less it costs and how much more or less effective it is.

In the example from Box 10.1, the new therapy was more expensive and more effective. This places it in Quadrant I (Option A in Fig. 10.1). A new drug that is less expensive and more effective appears in Quadrant IV (Option B in Fig. 10.1). In contrast, a therapy that is more expensive and less effective (Quadrant II, Option C) is clearly undesirable. The last option is a therapy that is cost saving but also less effective (located in quadrant III, option D in Fig. 10.1). There is no general rule for how to handle an alternative such as option D. Still, it is debatable whether we should adopt a new intervention that worsens health outcomes, even if it saves money.

One might argue that option D could be suitable for a specific subgroup of patients who are less severely affected and may not need the most effective (and expensive) treatment but could benefit from a less efficacious and also less costly drug. This, however, is a good example, underscoring the importance of defining the appropriate patient population when conducting a CEA. Considering only the subgroup of patients who are less severely affected, and assuming a similar effectiveness of the new drug in these less severely affected patients as with standard therapy,

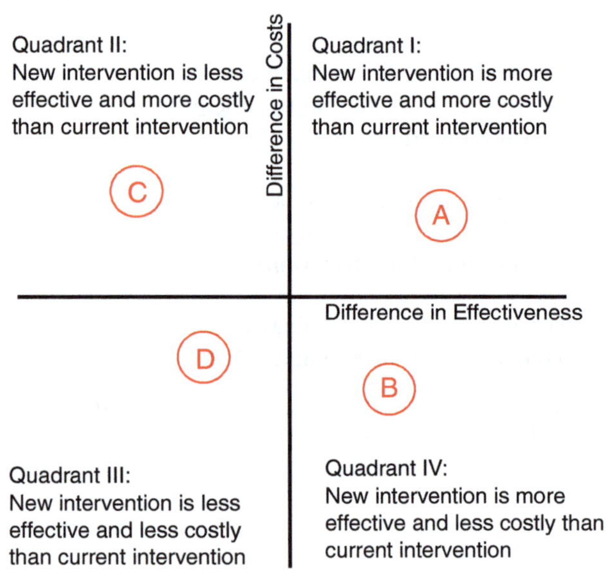

Fig. 10.1 Cost-effectiveness plane, depicting four different ICERs of a new therapy

the lower costs of the new drug will dominate the current treatment. However, this applies only to this subgroup of patients, thus limiting the use of the new drug to that specific group.

10.2.3 Commonly Used: Thresholds of Cost-Effectiveness

Returning to Option A from our earlier example with the new therapy being more effective but also more expensive, we now introduce the concept of cost-effectiveness thresholds. In human healthcare, budgets are limited in most countries and do not allow to adopt every new therapy regardless of cost. As a result, many countries have established threshold values, representing the maximum amount they are willing to pay for a specific health benefit, such as a life year gained or a QALY (the latter being the topic of Chap. 13). These thresholds vary by country and are used to decide whether a new intervention is considered cost-effective. In Fig. 10.2, this is illustrated using two diagonal green lines, a solid line and a dotted line, each representing a different country's threshold.

- A country with the lower threshold (solid green line) would consider only Option A_1 as cost-effective.
- A country with a higher threshold (dotted green line) might accept Options A_1 and A_2.
- Option A_3, being above both lines, would likely be considered too costly relative to its benefits in either case.

In veterinary medicine, however, there are no established cost-effectiveness thresholds, and it is unlikely that formal ones will be introduced. Decisions can vary

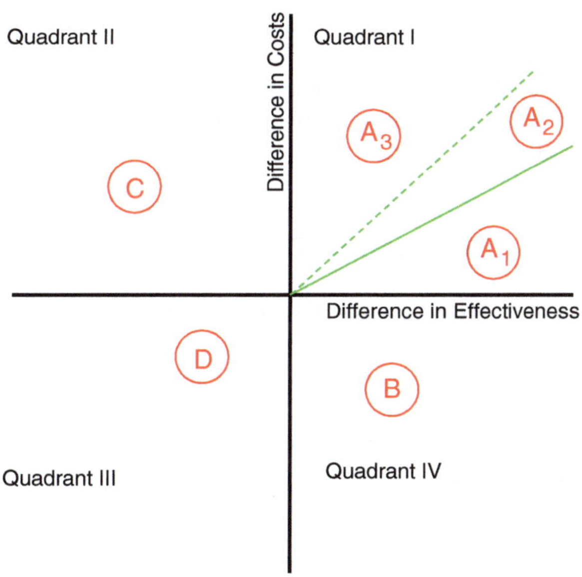

Fig. 10.2 Cost-effectiveness plane with two thresholds of incremental cost-effectiveness ratio, represented as solid and dotted green lines

widely depending on the animal species, the veterinary clinic, and particularly the animal owner. For the animal owner, it is not only a matter of willingness to pay but also of the ability to pay. Accordingly, the green lines in Fig. 10.2 will differ from one situation to another.

That said, in countries with widespread pet insurance, such thresholds could become more relevant. Insurers might define their own cost-effectiveness criteria to decide which treatments they are willing to cover, helping to manage costs while ensuring reasonable health outcomes for insured animals.

10.3 Main Approaches to CEA

After introducing the concept of cost-effectiveness analysis (CEA), the next step is to focus on the main approaches to CEA. A standard methodological approach is a decision or simulation model, with decision trees and Markov models being often used. These models will be described in detail in the following sections. Simple models can be built using MS Excel™; however, for more advanced models and analyses, multiple solutions exists, including R packages, MS Excel™ add-ins, or commercial software specifically developed for health care decision analysis.

Decision models, such as decision trees or Markov models allow the integration of data and information from diverse sources and can link marker or surrogate endpoints to patient-relevant outcomes. Additionally, they are often designed to simulate outcomes over extended time horizons, which go beyond the durations typically considered in clinical studies.

▶ Short Note on Model Types:
Decision trees and Markov models are both so-called stochastic models, i.e., they use probabilities which allow for the consideration of variability in outcomes. This makes stochastic models especially useful in CEA, where outcomes and costs are rarely certain or constant. In contrast, dynamic models focus on simulating time-dependent processes and are mainly used in animal health care to describe disease transmission processes. As such, dynamic models are beyond the scope of this book.

10.4 The Decision Tree

10.4.1 How Is a Decision Tree Structured?

A decision tree is much simpler than a Markov model, but it is a very useful and intuitive tool to display simple disease and treatment processes. Firstly, we will describe the structure of the tree (Figs. 10.3a–c). The path in a decision tree always runs from left to right:

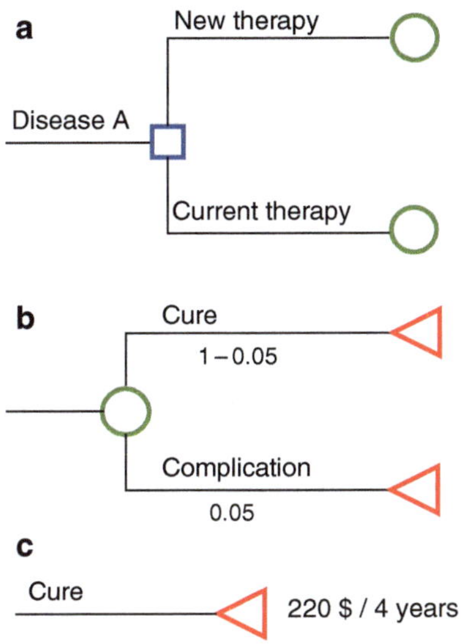

Fig. 10.3 (**a**) The tree starts at the trunk, often indicating the disease that should be evaluated. The first node is a so-called decision node (presented as square) and represents the decision being addressed in the model, i.e., in our example using the new or current therapy. (**b**) The following nodes are so-called chance nodes (presented as circles) and represent the points where clinical events are weighted by their probability of occurrence. Each of the alternatives must have a probability, which are conventionally placed below the path, and the probabilities originating from a single chance node must sum up to 1 (corresponding to 100%). (**c**) The last (triangular) node is the so-called terminal node representing the end of the branch. The data right to the node indicate the costs and health effects (here: average treatment costs accrued and life years gained for patients virtually passing through the decision tree up to this respective terminal node)

10.4.2 How to Analyze Decision Trees?

The last step is the analysis, also known as rollback (or fold-back) of the tree. A step-by-step calculation is provided in Box 10.2. In brief, the tree is always rolled back from right to left. At each chance node, the outcomes, costs, and health effects, are multiplied by their associated probabilities. These weighted outcomes are then added together for each branch. This process ultimately leads to the summary result: the Incremental Cost-Effectiveness Ratio (ICER) for the so-called base case analysis. In base case analysis, the results are calculated using the default input values for costs and health effect, as such differing from sensitivity analyses, where input parameters are varied to assess the robustness of the results (see Chap. 11 for more information).

In Box 10.2, we illustrate the calculations, using the same example that was the basis for the ICER calculation in Box 10.1. Although real-world decision trees are often much more complex, this simplified example serves to demonstrate the core principles.

Box 10.2 Example of a CEA Using a Decision Tree

We assume the following fictive and simplified situation (which was also basis for our example in Box 10.1):

- Disease A is a dreaded disease in cats. Although treatment exists that can cure the cat, an often deadly complication can develop despite therapy, which also reduces the life expectancy in surviving cats.
- A new therapy has been developed that reduces the probability of complication. However, in case of complication, the risk of dying and the reduced life expectancy is not affected by the new drug. From clinical studies the following probabilities have been defined:
  - Probability of complication with new drug 5%
  - Probability of complication with current drug 25%
  - Probability of death in case of complication 60%
  - Life expectancy after successful therapy without complication 4 years
  - Life expectancy after successful therapy of complication 1.5 years

The corresponding decision tree looks like this:

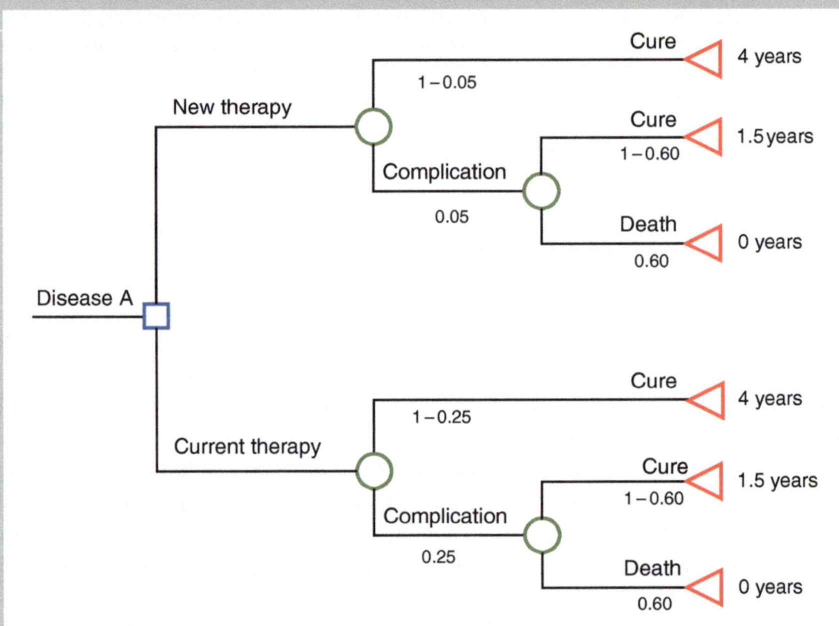

(continued)

Box 10.2 (continued)

The effectiveness (average life expectancy) can be calculated by "rolling back" the tree, i.e., for each branch the life expectance is multiplied by its probability, with results for all branches being summed up in the end:

New therapy:	(0.95 × 4 years + 0.05 × (0.40 × 1.5 years + 0.60 × 0 years) = 3.83 years
Current therapy:	(0.75 × 4 years + 0.25 × (0.40 × 1.5 years + 0.60 × 0 years) = 3.15 years

In order to finalize our decision tree, we still have to add the costs, which were defined as follows:

Cost of new therapy	220 USD
Cost of current therapy	60 USD
Cost of treating the complication	450 USD

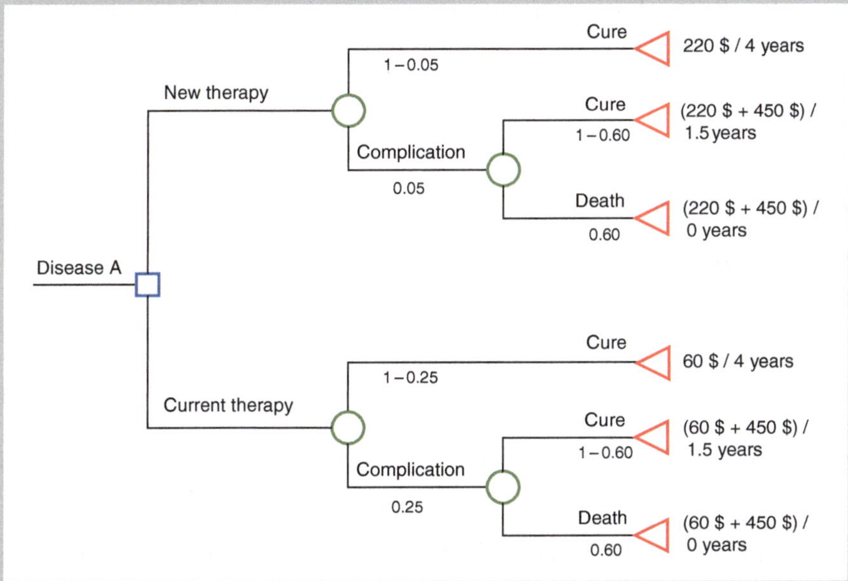

The cost data have been added to the decision tree which is now complete. The average costs can be calculated by "rolling back" the tree as described for effectiveness:

New therapy:	(0.95 × 220 $ + 0.05 × (0.40 × 670 $ + 0.60 × 670 $) = 242.50 $
Current therapy:	(0.75 × 60 $ + 0.25 × (0.40 × 510 $ + 0.60 × 510 $) = 172.50 $

And finally, the ICER is calculated, considering the costs and effectiveness as calculated:

$$(242.50\$ - 172.50\$) / (3.83 - 3.15\,\text{years}) = 70\$ / 0.68\,\text{years}$$

=> *One additional life year gained with the new drug costs USD 102.94.*

In human health care, an incremental cost of about USD 100 per life-year gained would sit far below the commonly used cost-effectiveness thresholds in upper-middle- and high-income countries [7], so the intervention would be considered highly cost-effective. In feline medicine, however, there is no formal threshold. Whether a cost of this magnitude is deemed acceptable depends on individual veterinarians' recommendations and on cat owners' willingness or ability to pay; some may see it as high, while others may readily adopt the new therapy.

10.4.3 What Are the Limitations of Decision Trees?

Although decision trees are widely used in human and animal health economic analyses, they have an important limitation. Because decision trees calculate costs and outcomes over a discrete time period, they are not well suited to model events that recur over time, which is often the case with chronic diseases. This limitation is addressed by Markov models, which will be described in the next section. In theory, also chronic diseases involving recurrent events could be modeled using a decision tree. However, these trees would be extremely complex, as every possible combination of events had to be included as single branch, making the tree very "bushy".

10.5 The Markov Model

10.5.1 What Is a Markov Model?

Markov models are also called state-transition models and represent a fundamental tool in cost-effectiveness analysis, particularly useful when health outcomes evolve over time. These models are ideally suited for chronic diseases or conditions with recurring events, where patients progress through various health states across multiple time periods. For instant, patients can progress through states of different disease severity, can be cured, or can die. The number and definition of the health states depend on the disease.

We will use a previously published Markov model [6] as basis for our example in Box 10.4. However, for a first acquaintance with Markov models, we have simplified the example. In Fig. 10.4 you will find a bubble diagram, an often-used presentation form of Markov models.

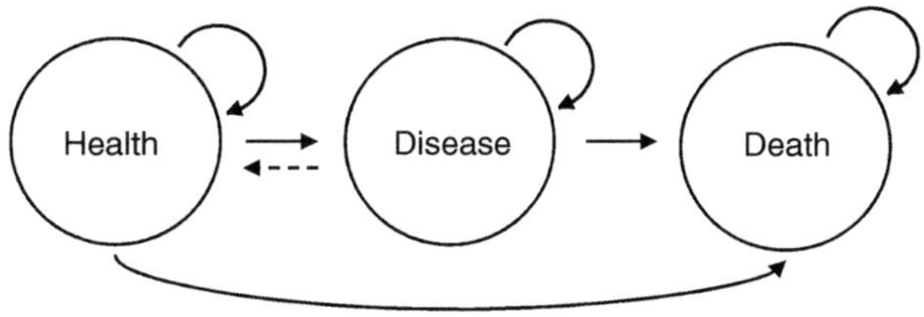

Fig. 10.4 Bubble diagram with three health states

In the simplified example, healthy patients can remain healthy (semicircular arrow line), can develop disease, or can die directly. Diseased patients can be cured (dotted line, as this might not apply in chronic diseases), remain ill, or can die. Death is a so-called absorbing state, which patients cannot leave once entered.

10.5.2 What Is a Cycle in a Markov Model?

In a Markov model, the total time of evaluation is divided into specific time periods, called cycles. The duration of a cycle depends on the disease and may span days, months, or years. Within a cycle, a patient cannot be in more than one health state. If for example, data from clinical studies show that some patients would move within the time period of a cycle to another health state, then the cycle length is not appropriate and need to be shortened. At the end of a cycle, patients remain in the health state or move to another one. In so-called absorbing states, with "death" being a common example, patients remain for the rest of the evaluation time.

10.5.3 How to Determine the Moving Between Health States?

The distribution of patients to different health states will be defined by so-called transition probabilities. Each transition probability defines the proportion of patients in a health state who will move to another health state or remain in the current one. The transition probabilities vary between the alternative treatments considered in the model (otherwise the treatments had identical effectiveness and no cost-effectiveness evaluation would be necessary). Accordingly, the transition probabilities are critical parameters in a Markov model and need to be defined carefully. They are often calculated from outcomes of clinical trials.

Box 10.3 provides an example calculation for transition probabilities.

Box 10.3 Simple Example of How to Calculate Transition Probabilities

In this simplified example, we are modeling the progression of a chronic disease in animals, with three possible health states:

- State A—No disease
- State B—Symptomatic disease
- State C—Death (an absorbing state)

Our model will have monthly cycles.
Step 1: Data collection from clinical trial
A clinical trial followed 100 dogs with no disease (State A) for 1 month. At the end of that month:

- 80 dogs remained in State A
- 15 progressed to State B
- 5 died (moved to State C)

Step 2: Calculation of the transition probabilities
To calculate the monthly probabilities of transitioning from State A:

- Probability of staying in State A: 80/100 = 0.80
- Probability of moving to State B: 15/100 = 0.15
- Probability of dying (moving to State C): 5/100 = 0.05

10.5.4 How to Assign Outcomes and Costs?

For each health state, the health outcome and costs need to be determined. We will start with the health outcome, using "life year" as example. This outcome reflects the total time the animal remains alive. As such, all health states except death contribute to the accumulation of life years. The contribution from each state depends on the cycle length used in the model:

- If the cycle length is 1 year, each health state except death contributes one life year.
- If the cycle length is 1 month, each non-death health state contributes 1/12, summing up to one life year after 12 cycles.

Additionally, the costs that accrue in each health state must be defined, considering all interventions, such as treatments or diagnostic procedures, that are applied in the respective health state.

Finally, the costs and health effects will be added up for each virtual patient according to their time they spend in the respective health state. Whereas in decision trees costs and effects are weighted by their probabilities assigned to each path, in a Markov model, the outcomes are weighted by the time a patient spend in each health state, which is determined by the transition probabilities.

10.5.5 How Transferrable Are Results from CEAs?

We will briefly present a previously published study, evaluating the cost-effectiveness of a new drug compared to a commonly used generic comparator in dogs with myxomatous valve disease (MVD), as valid for Germany [6]. The main details are summarized in Box 10.4.

Box 10.4 A Markov Model Developed for Myxomatous Valve Disease (MVD) in Dogs, Comparing the Cost-Effectiveness of a New Drug with a Generic Alternative in Germany [6]

Methodology: The model structure was based on two randomized controlled trials and is illustrated using a simplified bubble diagram:

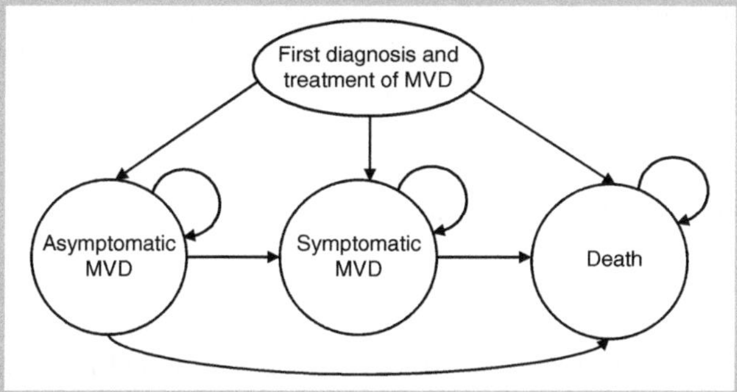

- Transition probabilities were calculated from the two clinical trials, complemented by expert opinion.
- Resource use associated with the treatment was derived from clinical studies and expert opinion.
- Costs were derived from official price and tariff lists.

Results: The new drug was found to be more expensive but also more effective, resulting in increased life expectancy compared to the generic alternative. The ICER was calculated at EUR 1.29 per additional life day gained. This places the result in Quadrant I of the cost-effectiveness plane, indicating higher cost and higher effectiveness.

The study estimated the cost of one additional life-day gained with the new drug at EUR 1.29. However, the model was populated with cost and resource-use data specific to Germany, meaning the results cannot be directly transferred to other countries. Since most drugs are marketed internationally, outcomes for other countries may also be of interest. This highlights another key advantage of health economic models: the ability to adapt them to different national contexts. In many cases, only the cost and resource-use inputs need to be updated for such adaptations.

Once the existing model is populated with country-specific data, a local ICER can be calculated. This was done in our example for Switzerland, where the mean cost per additional life-day was CHF 2.48 (equivalent to EUR 1.64, based on the average exchange rate at the time of the study), reflecting differences in national price structures [8].

Of course, if treatment patterns vary between countries, a new model need to be developed that reflects local peculiarities.

10.6 Cost-Utility Analysis

In human health care, another health economic analysis has been widely used: the cost-utility analysis. It can be regarded as special form of CEA, using the QALY (quality-adjusted life year) as outcome. This analysis has not been routinely introduced into veterinary medicine. However, since first attempts have been made to adapt the QALY-concept to animal health care, this outcome is described in detail in Chap. 13, which also provides an example of cost-utility analysis.

10.7 Drawbacks of the Models

No chapter on cost-effectiveness analysis (CEA) would be complete without acknowledging a key limitation of all health economic models: simplification. You may have already noticed that our Markov model simplified the treatment of disease, i.e., MVD in dogs. Indeed, every model is a simplification of a more complex reality. However, overly complex models can become less transparent, harder to interpret, and more dependent on assumptions, especially when data are limited or missing. This can undermine the model's credibility and usefulness. The key principle in designing a decision model is to make it no more complex than necessary to address the research question appropriately.

Take-Home Messages

- Cost-effectiveness analysis (CEA) is a systematic method for comparing two or more alternative interventions by calculating both their costs and health outcomes, ultimately expressing costs in relation to their effectiveness.
- The approach avoids placing a monetary value on health outcomes such as life years gained or improvements in quality of life.
- Results are typically presented as an incremental cost-effectiveness ratio (ICER), which reflects the additional cost required to gain one extra unit of health benefit, such as one additional life year, when comparing a new treatment to an existing one.
- Common modeling approaches in CEA include simple decision trees and more advanced Markov models, which are especially useful for estimating long-term outcomes as patients can move between different health states over time.

References

1. Rushton J, Gilbert W, Jones D (2018) A guide - introduction to the use of cost-effectiveness analysis in animal health. https://wwwgf-tadsorg/fileadmin/user_upload/gf-tads/docs/document_about/Global/CEA_Guide_Aug_2018pdf. Assessed 17 May 2025
2. Martins SB, Rushton J (2014) Cost-effectiveness analysis: adding value to assessment of animal health, welfare and production. Rev Sci Tech Off Int Epiz 33(3):681–689
3. Van Middelaar CE, Dijkstra J, Berentsen PBM, De Boer IJM (2014) Cost-effectiveness of feeding strategies to reduce greenhouse gas emissions from dairy farming. J Dairy Sci 97:2427–2439
4. Valeeva NI, Lam TJGM, Hogeveen H (2007) Motivation of dairy farmers to improve mastitis management. J Dairy Sci 90:4466–4477
5. Van Vlaenderen I, Poulsen Nautrup B, Gasper SM (2011) Estimation of the clinical and economic consequences of non-compliance with antimicrobial treatment of canine skin infections. Prev Vet Med 99:201–210
6. Poulsen Nautrup B, Van Vlaenderen I, Poulsen Nautrup C (2010) Pharmacoeconomic evaluation of the treatment of myxomatous mitral valve disease in dogs in Germany. Kleintierpraxis 55:184–195
7. Pichon-Riviere A, Drummond M, Palacios A, Garcia-Marti S, Augustovski F (2023) Determining the efficiency path to universal health coverage: cost-effectiveness thresholds for 174 countries based on growth in life expectancy and health expenditures. Lancet Glob Health 11:e833–e842
8. Poulsen Nautrup B, Van Vlaenderen I (2009) Cost-effectiveness of pimobendan versus benazepril in acquired myxomatous mitral valve disease in dogs: an adaptation to Switzerland. Value Health 12:A62

Sensitivity Analysis

11

Abstract

Sensitivity analyses (SAs) are an essential tool in health economic analyses. They help explore how uncertainties in input parameters can affect the results. A SA involves varying model parameters across a plausible range and recalculating the outcomes to assess whether conclusions stay the same. Common approaches include scenario analysis, deterministic SA, and probabilistic SA. Scenario analyses often use best-case/worst-case settings or study-specific scenarios. One of the most widely used deterministic SAs is the one-way SA, where only one parameter is changed at a time while the other parameters are kept constant, thereby quantifying the single parameter's impact on the outcome. This procedure is repeated for all parameters selected for SA. Results are often presented as tornado diagram, which visually ranks the most influencing parameters. Probabilistic SAs are a more complex approach, as the parameters are not assigned fixed values, but distributions, resulting in a range of possible inputs. The model is then run multiple times (e.g., 1000 or 10,000 times) to generate a range of outcomes. This method is called Monte Carlo simulation and results are often displayed as scatterplot, visualizing the results for the repeated simulations.

Keywords

Sensitivity analysis · Uncertainty · Scenario analysis · Deterministic sensitivity analysis · One-way sensitivity analysis · Probabilistic sensitivity analysis · Tornado diagram · Scatterplot

B. Poulsen Nautrup, *Outcomes Research in Animal Health Care*,
https://doi.org/10.1007/978-3-032-12587-3_11

In the previous chapters, we described different types of health economic studies. Regardless of the type, all of them rely on data inputs that are often uncertain to some degree. Sensitivity analysis (SA) is an essential tool in health economic analyses, evaluating how these uncertainties affect the conclusions drawn from economic evaluations.

11.1 Sources of Uncertainty

Health economic analyses commonly recognize three types of uncertainty: parameter uncertainty, structural uncertainty, and stochastic uncertainty. Table 11.1 provides an overview of these types. While most can be addressed through SA, structural uncertainty typically requires modifications to the model itself and is therefore not the focus of this chapter.

► Short Note:
Many guidelines, including Briggs et al. 2012 [1], present heterogeneity alongside the classical uncertainties because of its policy relevance, but in the strict sense used here, we did not list heterogeneity that reflects variability, rather than true uncertainty.

In the following, we will focus on the lack of certainty of input parameters, i.e., costs and effectiveness.

- *Cost data*: As outlined in Chap. 6, costs are composed of both unit prices and resources used. Even though drug prices or veterinary fees may be derived from official price or tariff lists, veterinarians often have some flexibility in pricing. Therefore, prices can vary between clinics. Similarly, resource use, such as the number of consultations or diagnostic procedures, can differ across regions and clinics. An additional factor applies particularly to dogs: the body weight varies relevantly across breeds, significantly influencing daily therapy costs.

  In health economic models that extrapolate outcomes over several years, costs must be discounted as described in Chap. 6, but there is no universal agreement on the appropriate discount rate and different rates can lead to different results, which need to be captured in SA.

Table 11.1 Sources of uncertainty in health economic analysis

Type of uncertainty	Definition	Example
Parameter uncertainty	Uncertainty in the numerical values used as model inputs	Variations in effectiveness and costs
Structural uncertainty	Uncertainty about the model structure and assumptions	Choice of model type (e.g., decision tree vs. Markov model)
Stochastic uncertainty	Random variations in outcomes between identical patients	Two identical animals respond differently to the same treatment

Table adapted from [1]

- *Effectiveness*: These parameters also contain uncertainty. For example, controlled clinical trial data often measure efficacy (i.e., performance under ideal conditions) rather than effectiveness (performance in real-world settings). In Chap. 3, we have outlined the difference between efficacy and effectiveness. In short, experimental study designs with a strict monitoring, patient management, and inclusion and exclusion criteria can result in outcomes that do not reflect the impact of a health intervention in daily practice.

  Furthermore, health economic models usually rely on mean or median values for base-case analyses, whereas effectiveness varies across individual animals. Most likely not all breeds, age groups, or animals with comorbidities are included in clinical trials, introducing further uncertainty as outcomes might vary across different groups.

11.2 Parameters and Ranges for SA

In SA, input parameters are varied across plausible ranges, and the results are recalculated. But which parameters should be changed and what is a plausible range for use in SA? There is more than one answer for each question.

11.2.1 Which Parameters Should Be Included in SA?

Ideally, all parameters should be subject to SA. In very complex models, however, it might be appropriate to limit the number of parameters, i.e., focusing on those parameters that are likely to affect results significantly.

11.2.2 What Ranges Should Be Used in SA?

There are several approaches to define parameter ranges for SA, including:

- *95% Confidence Interval (CI)*: This option is commonly used, especially for parameters derived from clinical trial data.
- *Fixed percentage range*: If no empirical data is available, a fixed range can be applied. A range of ±20% has been used in CEAs in animals, i.e., varying all parameters from 80% to 120% of their original value.
- *Minimum and maximum values from source data*: Where available, the lowest and highest reported values of the original data sources can be used to define the range.
- *Minimum and maximum possible values*: When parameter uncertainty is especially high, such as for assumptions, using the entire possible range may be appropriate.

Ranges can be applied uniformly across all parameters (e.g., a fixed range of ±20%). Alternatively, they can vary by parameter type, for instance, using 95% CIs for effectiveness parameters and fixed ranges for cost data. In all cases, the chosen ranges must be clearly documented and justified.

11.3 General Interpretation of SA

If the overall conclusion does not change relevantly in appropriate SA, the model is considered "robust." If varying a parameter leads to a major change, such as the shifting to a different quadrant in the cost-effectiveness plane, the model is said to be "sensitive" to that parameter. These parameters need special attention when interpreting results of a health economic analysis.

▶ Short Note:
The cost-effectiveness plane is described in detail in Chap. 10. In short, the cost-effectiveness plane depicts graphically the main outcome of a CEA, i.e., if the health intervention under investigation is more costly and more effective, more costly and less effective, less costly and more effective, or less costly and less effective than the treatment which serves as comparator. The four different outcome options are located in the four quadrants of the cost-effectiveness plane.

11.4 Different Types of SA

Health-economic evaluations usually report three headings for sensitivity analyses: deterministic analyses, probabilistic analyses, and scenario analyses. Strictly speaking, scenario analyses belong under the deterministic umbrella, but guidelines often list them separately because they test bundled assumptions rather than single-parameter ranges. Following that convention, we also treat scenario analysis as a distinct tool for examining uncertainty.

11.4.1 Which Scenarios Are Appropriate in SA?

One common form is the *best-case/worst-case scenario*, where parameters are set to their most favorable or unfavorable values. In the best-case scenario, the treatment under evaluation is assumed to have the best possible outcome and lowest costs, while all parameters for the comparator(s) are set at worst. In the worst-case scenario, this is reversed, i.e., to the disadvantage of the new intervention and advantage to the comparator. It should be noted, however, that the best-case/worst-case scenarios might not represent a realistic option, but show the most extreme outcomes within the predefined ranges.

Scenario analysis can also be tailored to specific model situations. In the previously presented model, assessing treatment for mitral valve disease (MVD) in dogs (Box 10.4 of Chap. 10) [2], two scenario analyses were included:

- *Scenario 1*: Treatment costs were recalculated for the smallest and largest dogs included in clinical studies, while efficacy was assumed to be similar in dogs of different weights.
- *Scenario 2*: The analysis compared outcomes for dogs treated with or without furosemide, a commonly recommended co-treatment of MVD at the time of study. This analysis evaluated the outcomes in both guideline-adherent and real-world practices.

11.4.2 What Is a Deterministic SA?

Common deterministic SA include one-way, two-way, and multi-way SAs, with one-way SA being the most popular option.

In *one-way SA*, the value of one single parameter is varied at a time, while others remain constant. This reveals how much each single parameter influences the outcome. Results are typically displayed in a tornado diagram, where each parameter's impact is shown as horizontal bar. The wider the bar, the more important is the parameter in terms of its potential effect on the overall outcome. The widest bar is presented at the top and the narrowest at the bottom of the tornado diagram, resulting in a funnel-like appearance [3].

Before presenting a previously published example in Box 11.1, we will explain in Fig. 11.1 the general structure of tornado diagrams.

In the example in Fig. 11.1, results correspond to the difference in profit with two alternative treatments, with positive values corresponding to a net profit with the treatment under investigation. In base case, the net profit (difference in costs) is calculated to USD 2 (easily detectable in Fig. 11.1, as it represents the border between results for minimum values (dark gray) and maximum values (light gray). The threshold value of USD 0 is marked in Fig. 11.1 by a red line.

In this example, 9 parameters are varied over a defined range, from which parameter 3 has the greatest impact on the results, closely followed by parameter 9. The parameters 3, 9, and 6 result in a reverse of outcome as the positive base case result

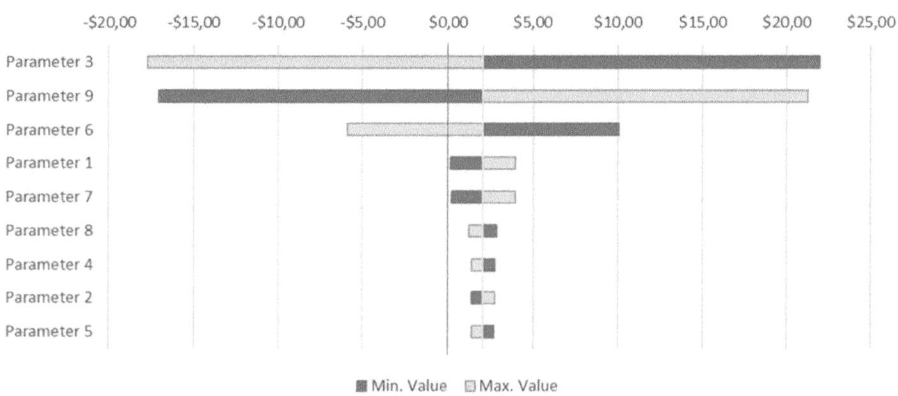

Fig. 11.1 General structure of a tornado diagram

becomes negative. The underlying model can be regarded as sensitive to these parameters. On the contrary, the other parameters included in the one-way SA have a lower (parameters 1 and 7) or negligible impact (parameters 8, 4, 2, and 5) on outcomes.

There is another aspect that should be noted with tornado diagrams: the minimum and maximum values can result in more positive or negative outcomes (as the dark and light gray bars can be on the right or left of the baseline value), depending on the impact of the parameter for the outcome, i.e., being in favor or disfavor for the treatment of choice. This helps illustrate whether a change in parameter favors or harms the intervention's outcome.

▶ Short Note on Threshold or Break-Even Analysis:
Threshold or break-even analysis addresses a straightforward, practical question: "By how much could a key parameter change before my decision would reverse?". Rather than varying all inputs across ranges, this approach focuses on a single, influential parameter, often identified using a tornado diagram, and calculates the exact value at which the result equals zero. In the example in Fig. 11.1, this critical point is represented by a red line, indicating a net profit of zero, i.e., no difference in profit between the two treatments.

Now we will come to a real-world example. In Box 11.1, part of the results of a one-way SA is presented, which have been reported in a previously published study that investigated key drivers of profitability in finishing pigs when implementing an immunization strategy [4].

Box 11.1 Example of a One-Way SA Based on a Previously Published Study [4]
In this study, a health economic model was used to identify key drivers of profitability in finishing pigs when implementing an immunization strategy.

The tornado diagram displays results for male pigs as relevant for producers in one country:

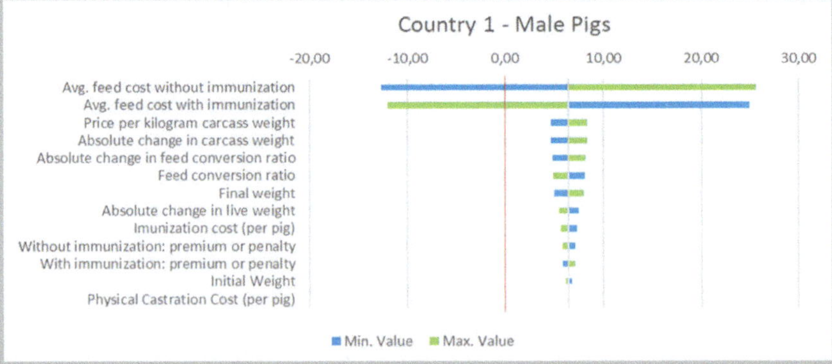

The tornado diagram shows that the model was only sensitive to feed costs, which were applied separately for pigs with and without immunization strategy. The other parameters considered in the model had a negligible impact on the overall profitability.

The SA presented in Box 11.1 is a good example for the main drawback of one-way SA. Although being very useful to identify the parameters with the greatest impact on the model's results, a disadvantage of one-way SA is that correlated parameters are changed unrelated to each other. In our example in Box 11.1, the costs of feed for pigs with immunization strategy and pigs with comparative intervention were considered separately, although it could be rationally assumed that changes in feed costs would apply to both groups of pigs.

To overcome this disadvantage, *two-way SAs* are often used, changing the related parameters simultaneously. This was also done in the published study where feed costs were changed simultaneously for pigs with and without immunization strategy. In our example country, the outcome no longer reversed the overall statement, i.e., did no longer cross the zero point of profitability. Expectedly, the parameter feed cost has become relevantly less impacting when changes were considered in both groups of animals.

In a *multi-way SA*, more than two parameters are varied simultaneously. However, with an increasing number of inputs that are varied, the SA becomes progressively more difficult to present and interpret. Therefore, multi-way SAs are less commonly used.

11.4.3 What Are Probabilistic SAs Used For?

The probabilistic SA (PSA) is a more complex approach for quantifying the uncertainty compared to deterministic SA. The basic concept involves two main aspects:

- *Assigning distributions*: the parameters are not assigned a certain value, but a distribution, resulting in a range of possible values rather than a fixed value.
- *Running simulations repeatedly*: the model is run repeatedly, e.g., 1000 or 10,000 times. It corresponds to virtual animals moving through the model, one after the other, which is called Monte Carlo simulation.

As the probabilities and costs are assigned a distribution rather than a fixed value, it is rather unlikely that two consecutive animals will be assigned the same probability at each decision node or the same cost per health state, resulting in different outcomes for each patient, thereby reflecting real-life variability. Of course, if the model is run often enough, by chance two virtual patients may come up with the same result.

We will start with the concept of assigning a distribution rather than a fixed value to the parameters. Although other distributions are used more often in CEA, we will explain the concept for a normal distribution, being the most well-known distribution.

In Fig. 11.2, the standard normal distribution around the base case value is depicted. Each time a virtual animal reaches a decision point in the model, a value is drawn from the assigned distribution. In the example of a normal distribution, values near base case value have a higher probability to be chosen, but less often

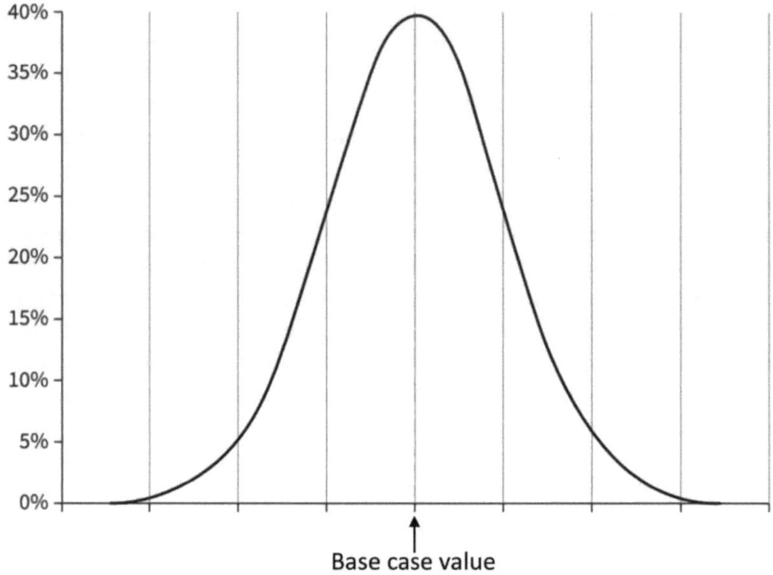

Fig. 11.2 The standard normal distribution around a base case value

probabilities more distant from base case value are also selected. This happens for each probability being subject to PSA and for each cost parameter included in PSA.

As already mentioned, the normal distribution, albeit being a nice example for explanation, is not the preferred distribution for all parameters. While it can be appropriate, for example, for average daily weight gain in pigs, it is less appropriate for probabilities and costs.

- *Probabilities* can only have a value between 0 and 1 (corresponding to 0% and 100%) and a beta-distribution is often used as it accounts for the peculiarity.
- *Cost data* cannot be negative, making them good candidates for a gamma distribution.

Regardless of the distribution(s) used, it is important to report and justify the distribution(s) used.

Which brings us to the point how to present the results from PSA? The most common presentation is a scatterplot. Each virtual animal passing through the model is depicted as one point, resulting in an accumulation of points. An example of a scatterplot from a published cost-effectiveness analysis is provided in Box 11.2.

Box 11.2 Cost-Effectiveness Scatterplot

In this example, a scatterplot has been created with each point representing the result (cost in relation to the health effect) for one animal from 10,000 patients virtually passing through the model.

The example shows the outcome of the probabilistic sensitivity analysis run for a CEA, evaluating the cost-effectiveness of a patented drug (light green points) and a generic drug (blue point) for treatment of mitral valve disease in dogs.

Cost-effectiveness scatterplot (re-run and adapted from a published cost-effectiveness study [5]):

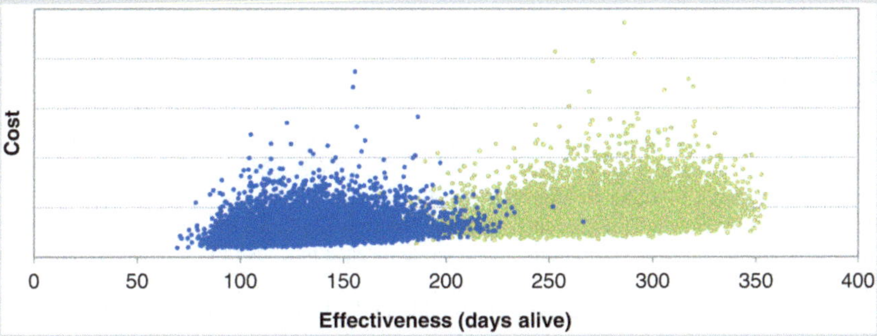

Results:

The patented drug (light green dots)

- caused slightly higher costs, as the cluster of simulations is a little higher than that for the comparator (blue dots)
- was more effective in terms of life expectancy, as the cluster is to the right of that for the comparator drug

▶ Short Note:
In human medicine, PSA is often used to create an acceptability curve, i.e., to estimate how many of the virtual patients would be assigned an outcome below a defined threshold, defining, for example, the maximum acceptable costs for an additional life year gained. However, in animal healthcare, universally accepted thresholds are missing and this approach is not yet standard practice.

In conclusion, PSA is used to account for uncertainty in input parameters such as costs and effectiveness. By assigning probability distributions to these parameters and running repeated simulations, PSA captures how uncertainty of the input data influences the overall results.

Take-Home Messages

- Sensitivity analyses are essential in health economic evaluations to explore how uncertainty in input parameters affects model results.
- Scenario analyses are useful for exploring different possible situations, such as best-case or worst-case scenarios, or to compare alternative assumptions about how a treatment is used in practice.
- Deterministic sensitivity analyses, such as one-way SAs, help identify which individual parameters have the greatest influence on outcomes.
- Probabilistic sensitivity analyses offer a more comprehensive view by incorporating uncertainty across multiple parameters simultaneously, providing a more realistic estimate of variability and decision uncertainty.

References

1. Briggs AH, Weinstein MC, Fenwick EAL, Karnon J, Sculpher MJ, Paltiel AD (2012) Model parameter estimation and uncertainty: a report of the ISPOR-SMDM modeling good research practices task force-6. Value Health 15:835–842
2. Poulsen Nautrup B, VanVlaenderen I, Poulsen Nautrup C (2010) Pharmacoeconomic evaluation of the treatment of myxomatous mitral valve disease in dogs in Germany. Kleintierpraxis 55:184–195
3. Drummond MF, Sculpher MJ, Claxton K, Stoddart GL, Torrance GW (2015) Methods for the economic evaluation of health care programmes, 4th edn. Oxford University Press, Oxford
4. Poulsen Nautrup B, Van Vlaenderen I, Mah CK, Aldaz A (2024) Using an economic simulation model to identify key drivers of profitability and estimate the environmental sustainability impact of immunization against gonadotropin-releasing factor (GnRF) in male and female pigs intended for market. Res Vet Sci 168:105154
5. Poulsen Nautrup B, Van Vlaenderen I (2009) Cost-effectiveness of pimobendan versus benazepril in acquired myxomatous mitral valve disease in dogs: an adaptation to Switzerland. Value Health 12:A62

Part IV

Quality of Life and Animal Welfare

Quality of life and animal welfare are core areas of OR; therefore, an entire part of this book has been dedicated to this important aspect.

In Chap. 12, we will present the different options to measure quality of life and animal welfare. Chapters 13 and 14 deal with the health-adjusted life years, which allow the combined consideration of mortality and morbidity, with the life years being weighted by their health-related quality. The two most common measures within the group of health-adjusted life years are the quality-adjusted life years (QALYs) and disability-adjusted life years (DALYs). QALYs have been mainly developed for use in cost-effectiveness analyses, evaluating the most appropriate health intervention in terms of costs and outcomes for the patient, whereas DALYs were developed to quantify the burden of disease. Both measures are valuable tools to support resource allocation in the human health sector. As both concepts have been recently adapted for use in animals, it is worth to take a closer look at the two measures, which have the potential to relevantly support the consideration of QoL in animal health care decisions.

12 Quality of Life and Animal Welfare

Abstract

There is no universally accepted definition of quality of life (QoL) or welfare in animals. While the terms are sometimes used interchangeably, they are often treated as distinct concepts. The “Five Freedoms” have long served as a basis for assessing animal welfare, especially in livestock, while QoL is a term more commonly used in companion animal care, focusing on the animal’s subjective experience. Research has shown that veterinarians tend to better assess medical or pain-related aspects of welfare, whereas animal caretakers often have better insight into the animal’s psychological state, suggesting the benefit of combining the two perspectives. Validated questionnaires are essential for thorough evaluations, as they account for the many dimensions of QoL or welfare. Generally, questionnaires can be classified into two main types: disease-specific tools and generic instruments. Disease-specific questionnaires can detect small changes in animals with a certain disease, while generic instruments are less sensitive but can be used in animals, regardless of their health status. In human medicine, generic instruments have been developed that convert QoL into a single numerical value, also called “utility.” One of these instruments has been preliminarily created for use in dogs, i.e., the “dog health utility index.”

Keywords

Quality of life · Animal welfare · Disease-specific questionnaires · Index questionnaires · Dog health utility index · Proxy assessment · Five Freedoms · Utility · Health states · Disability paradox

B. Poulsen Nautrup, *Outcomes Research in Animal Health Care*,
https://doi.org/10.1007/978-3-032-12587-3_12

Quality of life (QoL) and animal welfare are core aspects of outcomes research (OR). They play an increasingly important role in decision-making at all levels, from governments and international organizations, to herd or farm management, or when it comes to treatment decisions in a single animal or to define the appropriate time for euthanasia.

Accordingly, in recent decades, attention to animal QoL and welfare has grown significantly. This has led to the development of numerous measurement tools, particularly for dogs and cats, though their application in daily practice remains limited. In livestock, considerations of animal welfare are also becoming more important, reflecting growing public and industry interest. However, there are still challenges that need to be overcome before animal QoL receives the same level of attention as QoL in human medicine.

12.1 Definitions

This chapter starts with a definition of QoL and animal welfare, which is not an easy task, as no commonly accepted definition exists.

Whereas QoL and animal welfare are sometimes used interchangeably, many scientists differentiate between the two concepts and often associate QoL with pets and welfare with livestock.

12.1.1 What Characterizes QoL?

The QoL concept is inspired by human psychology and medicine and focuses on how the individual perceives its own welfare state. It can be described as a balance between an animal's negative and positive experiences over time. However, a generally agreed upon definition is missing and often hinders the comparability of assessments. If studies use different definitions, they measure different aspects and outcomes might not be comparable.

One comprehensive definition is:

> *QoL is the state of an individual animal's life as perceived by them at any one point in time. It is experienced as a sense of well-being which involves the balance between negative and positive affective states and any cognitive evaluation of these, where the animal has the capacity. To some extent, QoL can be predicted by the fulfilment of basic and species-specific health, social and environmental needs (and individual preferences for these) and is reflected in their health and behavior* [1].

Another, shorter version defines QoL as "an individual's satisfaction with its physical and psychological health, its physical and social environment and its ability to interact with that environment" [2].

Both definitions emphasize that QoL is more than just physical health or the absence of pain, as it includes psychological and social factors. Tools that measure QoL should take its complexity into account.

12.1.2 What Distinguishes Animal Welfare from QoL?

Like QoL, there is no single agreed-upon definition of animal welfare. One widely known framework is the "Five Freedoms" [3], which has provided a basis for many welfare measurements, especially in livestock.

The "Five Freedoms" have been summarized in Box 12.1.

Box 12.1: The *Five Freedoms* [3]

1. Freedom from hunger and thirst—by ready access to fresh water and a diet to maintain full health and vigor.
2. Freedom from discomfort—by providing an appropriate environment including shelter and a comfortable resting area.
3. Freedom from pain, injury, or disease—by prevention or rapid diagnosis and treatment.
4. Freedom to express normal behavior—by providing sufficient space, proper facilities, and company of the animal's own kind.
5. Freedom from fear and distress—by ensuring conditions and treatment which avoid mental suffering.

▶ Important Note:
For reasons of simplicity, we will use the term QoL in the following sections for both concepts.

12.2 Assessing QoL

12.2.1 Who Should Assess QoL in Animals?

In human medicine, QoL is ideally self-reported, since it is considered a subjective experience, as such representing a real patient-reported outcome. However, young children and individuals with cognitive impairments may not be able to complete a questionnaire or answer to corresponding questions. In such cases, a so-called "proxy" is required, such as the clinician, the parents, or care takers. Obviously, in veterinary medicine we always need a human proxy. This may be the animal owner, a farm manager, the veterinarian or veterinary nurse, or any other person involved in the care of the animal. In rare cases or in a research setting, also animal behaviorists or trained observers can be assigned with the task.

As outlined in the following, a joint evaluation carried out by different proxies might provide a more comprehensive view than a single assessment, as each proxy has strengths and limitations.

For instance, an owner who spends a lot of time with the animal may better recognize subtle behavioral or emotional changes. Veterinarians, on the other hand, are generally more skilled in assessing health or pain levels. This complementary knowledge suggests that combining input from the owner and the veterinarian can provide a more thorough picture of the animal's QoL. However, coordinating both perspectives can be time-consuming, and lack of time is a major reason why QoL questionnaires are not more widely used in day-to-day practice [4].

Some owners might overestimate an animal's QoL because they are responsible for the animal's well-being. In human medicine, the "disability paradox" describes cases where individuals with severe health problems or disabilities report a higher QoL than outside observers would expect. A similar phenomenon has been reported for animal care takers [5], reminding us that relying on just one perspective can sometimes be misleading. Additionally, a decline in QoL that develops gradually might be unnoticed by someone who is involved with the animal every day.

12.2.2 How to Approach QoL in Animals?

A very simple approach using a single question might already provide a rough estimate, for instance, *"How would you rate your animal's QoL on a scale between zero and 10, with zero being the worst possible QoL and 10 corresponding to perfect QoL?"*

However, for thorough evaluations, validated multi-dimensional QoL questionnaires should be used.

▶ Important Note
The validation of a questionnaire is critical to ensure that it measures what it claims to. Box 12.2 highlights some key validation criteria for QoL questionnaires. However, despite the importance of validation, many published studies in veterinary medicine use unvalidated or insufficiently validated questionnaires, thereby limiting the usefulness and transferability of outcomes [6].

Box 12.2: Some Validation Criteria for QoL Questionnaires (Excerpt Adapted from [6])

Measure	Test	What is assessed?
Reliability	Internal consistency	Do related questions yield similar results?
	Test-retest reliability	Are results stable over time, if no changes in the animal's condition have occurred?
	Inter-rater reliability	Do different assessors reach the same conclusions?
Validity	Content validity	Does the questionnaire cover all important aspects related to health or the disease?
	Construct validity	Do results align with established clinical evaluations?

Many existing questionnaires are paper-based, but increasingly also available as web tool or app for smartphones.

When used appropriately, these tools can support treatment or euthanasia decisions, as they can reduce the owner's emotional and personal bias in difficult decisions. Additionally, they support the communication between veterinarian and animal owner, increasing the treatment success and improving the understanding from the animal owner [5].

12.2.3 How Are QoL Questionnaire Structured?

Many QoL questionnaires are divided into domains or dimensions, which are further broken down into items. For example, a generic feline health-related QoL instrument has three domains, i.e., vitality, comfort, and emotional well-being, based on 20 items [7].

▶ Short Definition of Terms

The terms "domain" and "dimension" are often used interchangeably, as many questionnaires only differentiate between two levels of hierarchy. However, depending on the structure of the questionnaire, the following three levels of hierarchy can be found:

- The *Domains* are the broadest categories or areas of QoL being measured (e.g., physical health).
- The *Dimensions* represent specific subcategories or components within a domain (e.g., pain).
- The *Items* are individual questions or statements within the questionnaire that assess specific aspects of a dimension or domain (e.g., "Does the animal walk without difficulties?").

Although open-ended questions can offer deep insights into the health, well-being, and experiences, they are harder to analyze compared to structured responses and often require some kind of qualitative coding. Additionally, they are subject to response variability, as some respondents may give detailed answers, whereas others may respond very little.

For that reason, most QoL questionnaires rely on predefined response scales. Common examples include the Likert scale, Numerical Rating Scale (NRS), and Visual Analogue Scale (VAS). These scales are briefly described in Box 12.3.

Box 12.3: Common Scales in QoL Questionnaires

1. Likert Scale: Respondents choose from statements like "Strongly Disagree" to "Strongly Agree," typically on a 5- or 7-point scale.
2. Numerical Rating Scale (NRS): A numbered scale (e.g., 0–10 or 0–100) where respondents select a single number to represent their answer. For example, pain often should be rated on a scale from 0 (no pain) to 10 (worst pain imaginable).
3. Visual Analogue Scale (VAS): A continuous line (often 10 cm long) labeled at each end (e.g., "No pain" on the left and "Worst pain imaginable" on the right), where respondents mark a point, which can be measured in millimeters to assign a score.

12.2.4 What Are the Main Types of QoL Questionnaires?

There are two broad categories of QoL questionnaires: the disease-specific and generic questionnaires.

Disease-Specific Questionnaires

Disease-specific questionnaires are tailored for animals with a specific disease or condition. They focus on the so-called health-related aspects of QoL, i.e., disease aspects that impact the animal's QoL. For numerous diseases, quality of life questionnaires exist, such as chronic pain in dogs [8], cardiac disease in dogs [9] and cats [10], or respiratory disease in calves [11]. However, the list is only exemplarily and by far not exhaustive.

Disease-specific tools are highly sensitive and can detect small changes due to the disease or its treatment, which makes them popular in clinical research.

A potential drawback is the fact that comorbidities or treatment-related side effects might not be recognized by the questionnaires. Disease-specific questionnaires are the preferred tools in clinical studies, where changes in QoL due to a therapeutic intervention should be measured. In these studies, inclusion criteria often exclude patients with multiple diseases, thereby reducing the drawback of missing the impact of comorbidities. However, the missing recognition of side effects and comorbidities should always be kept in mind when using a disease-specific questionnaire in daily practice or for OR purposes.

Generic Tools

Generic QoL questionnaires or "holistic" instruments can be used in any animal, regardless of a potential health problem. Most of them are less sensitive than disease-specific questionnaires, but more robust when used in animals with comorbidities, such as geriatric pets nearing the end of their life. Additionally, generic tools allow comparisons over different patient groups and therapies. A review in 2020 identified nine generic QoL assessment tools (four designed for cats, four for dogs, and one for both) that met the defined inclusion and exclusion criteria [6]. For the use in chronically ill and geriatric horses, a Horse Welfare Assessment Tool has been developed [12]. Although not called "generic," several tools have been developed for use in livestock, based on the "Five freedoms." As these tools evaluate the general welfare, they can also be considered generic instruments. Examples are an Animal Welfare Assessment for Dairy farmers [13] and an instrument to measure QoL in farmed pigs [14].

12.2.5 How Are QoL Results Reported?

QoL results are often presented in three ways: as health profiles, a summary score, or an index.

(a) *Health profiles*: Here each domain is assessed separately and results are also presented separately for each domain. For instance, in the feline health-related QoL instrument mentioned earlier, results for vitality, comfort, and emotional wellbeing are shown as three separate scores [7]. Reporting the outcomes separately for different domains or dimensions is a common presentation of results from disease-specific questionnaires in human medicine.

(b) *Summary scores*: In veterinary medicine, some questionnaires produce a single score by adding up the answers. This is straightforward and easy to understand, but assumes that each domain or question has the same importance. In other words and using the example of the feline questionnaire, do changes in the domains vitality, comfort, and emotional well-being equally affect the QoL?

(c) *Index or utility instruments*: The last question brings us to the index instruments. In human medicine, some index instruments have been developed which account for different weights placed upon different dimensions, finally expressing the QoL in a single figure, often referred to as utility. Accordingly, the instruments are also called utility instruments and the calculated utility can be used in cost-effectiveness analysis, which are then called cost-utility analysis. It should be noted, however, that the task of transferring outcomes of questionnaires into a weighted figure is elaborate and resource consuming, and thereby has not been often applied in animal health care.

However, the option to use the utilities in cost-effectiveness analyses makes these instruments very valuable, explaining their widespread use for allocation decisions in human health care. The main index questionnaires in human medicine are the EuroQol 5-Dimension (EQ-5D), the Short Form 6 Dimensions (SF-6D), and the Health Utility Index (HUI). We will further describe these instruments for two reasons:

- These instruments provide an index figure, which can be used to calculate the quality-adjusted life year (QALY), the main outcome in human health economic analyses.
- The QALY-concept could also be very useful in animal health care for decision making, priority setting, and treatment comparisons. Accordingly, the first instrument, the HUI, has been preliminarily created for use in dogs: the Dog Health Utility Index (DHUI) [5]. Although a broader use of this new questionnaire would require further adaptations and validations, it represents a first step of introducing such an instrument in animal health care.

In Box 12.4, we present the dimensions of the three human index instruments together with the structure of the preliminarily developed DHUI.

▶ Important Note:
We will focus in this chapter on the index questionnaires and their peculiarities, whereas in Chap. 13, the application of their utilities in cost-effectiveness or cost-utility analyses will be described.

Box 12.4: Utility Instruments Developed for Use in Humans (Short Form 6 [SF-6], EuroQol 5-Dimension [EQ-5D-5L], Health Utility Index [HUI]) and Dogs (Dog Health Utility Index [DHUI]), Displaying the Dimensions and Number of Items Included per Dimension (in Brackets)

SF-6D [15]	EQ-5D-5L [16]	HUI 3 [17]	DHUI [5]
1. Physical functioning (6) 2. Role limitation (4) 3. Social functioning (5) 4. Pain (6) 5. Mental health (5) 6. Vitality (5)	1. Mobility (5) 2. Self-care (5) 3. Usual activities (5) 4. Pain/discomfort (5) 5. Anxiety/depression (5) VAS (of the health today)	1. Vision (6) 2. Hearing (6) 3. Speech (5) 4. Ambulation (6) 5. Dexterity (6) 6. Emotion (5) 7. Cognition (6) 8. Pain (5)	1. Pain (7) 2. Mobility (8) 3. Mental state (scale 1–10) 4. Cognition (scale 1–10)

▶ Short explanation

Using the DHUI as example, the table reads as follows: The DHUI has 4 dimensions: Pain, Mobility, Mental state, and Cognition. Pain and mobility contain 7 and 8 levels, respectively. For instance, in the dimension "pain," level 1 corresponds to "no pain or discomfort," level 2 corresponds to "occasional pain or discomfort," and the 7th level is "continuous severe and intense pain."

The dimensions "Mental state" and "Cognition" had to be rated on a scale between 1 and 10, with 1 being the worst state and 10 the best state imaginable [5].

It should be noted, however, that the DHUI still needs to be further adapted and validated for use in veterinary practice.

12.2.6 How Are Results Converted into One Figure?

The main challenge with index or utility questionnaires is converting the responses into a single score that reflects the overall QoL. In human healthcare, a representative sample of the general population is typically asked to assign values to various "health states" described by the questionnaire results. Asking the general population instead of people with certain disabilities helps determine how society at large values different levels of health or disability. Box 12.5 shows an example from the EQ-5D to illustrate the procedure.

Altogether, it is important to recognize that the final outcome, the index or utility, is evaluated considering health states rather than diseases.

Box 12.5: How to Convert the Outcomes from an Index Questionnaire into a Single Figure?

We will explain the general methodology using an example of the EuroQol 5-Dimension (EQ-5D).

The EQ-5D has five dimensions (mobility, self-care, usual activities, pain/discomfort, and anxiety/depression). For each dimension, five levels exists [16]:

- Level 1: no problems
- Level 2: slight problems
- Level 3: moderate problems
- Level 4: severe problems
- Level 5: extreme problems

A complete healthy patient would have a score of 1 1 1 1 1 (no problems in each of the five dimensions).

We will assume a patient has filled in the five dimensions as 2 1 3 3 1. That means, the patient has slight problems with mobility (Level 2), no problems with self-care (Level 1), moderate problems with general activities (Level 3), moderate pain (Level 3), and is not anxious or depressed (Level 1).

This description has been given to the population selected for evaluation who has rated the corresponding health state. The valuation is made for the EQ-5D, using the time trade-off method. However, for the HUI, the standard gamble technique has been used, which was initially also used for the SF-6D, but replaced by more scientific valuation approaches, which are, however, beyond the scope of this book. Regardless of the method, the final results correspond to the utility the general population assigns to that specific health state.

▶ Short Excursus:

- The *time trade-off* method evaluates how many years in perfect health an individual would be willing to give up in order to avoid living a longer period in the health state of interest, which is worse than perfect health.
- When using the *standard gamble*, an individual is given the choice between the health state under evaluation and a gamble with two possible outcomes: the best possible health (with probability p) and immediate death (with probability 1 − p). If the individual is indifferent when the gamble offers a 70% chance of full health and a 30% chance of death, the utility of their current health state is 0.7.

12.2.7 How Does the Dog Health Utility Index (DHUI) Work?

The DHUI, developed by Pesie (2012) [5], includes four dimensions: Pain, Mobility, Mental state, and Cognition, each weighted by its perceived importance to overall well-being. Therefore, included participants (veterinarians, animal scientists, and general population) distributed 100 points among the four dimensions to indicate their relative importance for QoL. The average weights were as follows: Mobility: 32.3%, Pain: 27.6%, Mental state: 22.8%, Cognition: 17.3%.

In the following, the participants were asked to assign utility scores from 1 to 10 to various levels within the two dimensions: Pain (7 levels) and Mobility (8 levels). These levels represent a spectrum of symptom severity (e.g., from "no pain" to "continuous severe pain"). Mental state and Cognition had to be scored directly by the proxy (e.g., the dog owner or vet) on a scale from 1 to 10, reflecting the animal's mental well-being and cognitive function at a given point.

In the end, each utility score is multiplied by its respective weight, and the products are summed to yield a single DHUI score:

$$\begin{aligned} \text{DHUI score} &= (\text{Mobility score} \times 0.323) + (\text{Pain score} \times 0.276) \\ &+ (\text{Mental state score} \times 0.228) + (\text{Cognition score} \times 0.173) \end{aligned}$$

This composite score represents the dog's overall quality of life on a continuous scale.

An example in Box 12.6 illustrates the process.

It should be noted, however, that the DHUI should be regarded as preliminary and still needs further adaptation and validation.

Box 12.6: Example of the Dog Health Utility Index (DHUI) (Adapted from Table 26 of [5])

The DHUI has four dimensions (Pain, Mobility, Mental state, and Cognition). For the first two attributes, 7 (pain) and 8 (mobility) levels have been defined and utility scores assigned to each level. The last two attributes are defined on a scale between 1 and 10.

The following table presents the results for a fictive dog, used as example in the reference [5]:

Attribute	Score	Weight	Contribution (score × weight)
Pain	2.48	27.6 %	0.685
Mobility	4.9	32.3 %	1.583
Mental state	5.0	22.8 %	1.140
Cognition	9.0	17.3 %	1.557
Total Score (2.48 * 0.276 + 4.9 * 0.323 + 5.0 * 0.228 + 9.0 * 0.173) = **4.96**			

- The example dog has a final score of 4.96 out of 10.
- The author defined the animal disease burden (ADB) as *Ideal QoL—Expected QoL*
- Accordingly, the ADB calculates to 10 − 4.96 = 5.04 for the fictive dog.

Take-Home Messages

- In veterinary medicine, a human proxy is always needed to assess an animal's QoL or welfare.
- Studies suggest that veterinarians are usually better at judging health or pain-related factors, while caretakers often recognize behavioral or emotional issues more accurately.
- Validated questionnaires, which cover the complex facet of QoL or welfare, are the gold standard for thorough assessment.
- Disease-specific questionnaires are developed for use in animals with specific diseases, whereas generic instruments are less sensitive but can be used in animals unrelated to any disease.
- Generic index instruments which can condense QoL into a single figure, the so-called utility, have been developed in human health care. One such tool has been preliminarily adapted for use in dogs, called the dog health utility index (DHUI).

References

1. Taylor K, Mills D (2007) Is quality of life a useful concept for companion animals? Anim Welf 16(S1):55–65
2. Belshaw Z, Asher L, Harvey ND, Dean RS (2015) Quality of life assessment in domestic dogs: an evidence-based rapid review. Vet J 206:203–212
3. World Organization for Animal Health. Animal Welfare.. https://www.woah.org/en/what-we-do/animal-health-and-welfare/animal-welfare/ Accessed 01 Jul 2025
4. Roberts C, Blackwell EJ, Roe E, Murrell JC, Mullan S (2023) Awareness and use of canine quality of life assessment tools in UK veterinary practice. Animals 13:1105
5. Pesie S (2012) Quantification of animal disease burden; exploring the possibilities of a dog-health utility index. Msc Thesis Wageningen University. https://library.wur.nl/WebQuery/theses/2016054. Assessed 01 Jul 2025
6. Fulmer AE, Laven LJ, Hill KE (2022) Quality of life measurement in dogs and cats: a scoping review of generic tools. Animals 12:400
7. Noble CE, Wiseman-Orr LM, Scott ME, Nolan AM, Reid J (2019) Development, initial validation and reliability testing of a web-based, generic feline health-related quality-of-life instrument. J Feline Med Surg 21(2):84–94
8. Brown DC, Boston RC, Coyne JC, Farrar JT (2007) Development and psychometric testing of an instrument designed to measure chronic pain in dogs with osteoarthritis. Am J Vet Res 68(6):631–637
9. Freeman LM, Rush JE, Farabaugh AE, Must A (2005) Development and evaluation of a questionnaire for assessing health-related quality of life in dogs with cardiac disease. J Am Vet Med Assoc 226:1864–1868
10. Freeman LM, Rush JE, Oyama MA, MacDonald KA, Cunningham SM, Bulmer B et al (2012) Development and evaluation of a questionnaire for assessment of health-related quality of life in cats with cardiac disease. J Am Vet Med Assoc 240:1188–1193
11. Bell DJ, Duthie C-A, Mason CS, Hancock A, Penny C, Odeyemi I et al (2024) Developing a tool to assess the health-related quality of life in calves with respiratory disease: tool refinement and construct validity testing. Animal 18:101215
12. Long M, Dürnberger C, Jenner F, Kelemen Z, Auer U, Grimm H (2022) Quality of life within horse welfare assessment tools: informing decisions for chronically Ill and geriatric horses. Animals 12:1822

13. Van Eerdenburg FJCM, Di Giacinto AM, Hulsen J, Snel B, Stegeman JA (2021) A new, practical animal welfare assessment for dairy farmers. Animals 11:881
14. Wiseman-Orr M, Scott E, Nolan A (2011) Development and testing of a novel instrument to measure health-related quality of life (HRQL) of farmed pigs and promote welfare enhancement (Part 1). Anim Welf 20:535–548
15. Mukuria C, Rowen D, Mulhern B, McDool E, Kharroubi S, Bjorner JB et al (2025) The Short Form 6 Dimensions (SF-6D): development and evolution. Appl Health Econ Health Policy 23:19–33
16. EuroQol. EQ-5D-5L (2009). https://euroqol.org/information-and-support/euroqol-instruments/eq-5d-5l/. Assessed 01 Jul 2025
17. Health Utilities Inc. HUI (2018). http://www.healthutilities.com/hui3.htm. Assessed 01 Jul 2025

Quality-Adjusted Life Years 13

Abstract

Quality-adjusted life year (QALY) is a widely used metric in human health economics that combines both quantity and quality of life into a single figure. A QALY is calculated by multiplying the time spent in a given health state by a utility representing the quality of this state, where 0 equals death and 1 represents perfect health. This allows the comparison of medical interventions regarding life expectancy and quality of life. QALYs are the basis of cost-utility analyses and support allocation decisions in human health care when resources are limited. While the concept has been extensively applied in human medicine, it has not been widely adopted in veterinary medicine yet. However, growing interest in animal welfare and quality of life has prompted researchers to explore how the QALY concept might be adapted for use in animals. The dog health utility index (DHUI) is an early step in creating a QALY-like measure that can be applied when evaluating treatments. If such tools would become validated and commonly used, they could offer valuable insights into which interventions provide the greatest benefit to companion animals and livestock, helping professionals set priorities and make informed decisions in animal health care.

Keywords

Health-adjusted life year · Quality-adjusted life year · QALY · Cost-utility analysis · Dog health utility index · Utility

B. Poulsen Nautrup, *Outcomes Research in Animal Health Care*,
https://doi.org/10.1007/978-3-032-12587-3_13

Quality-adjusted life years (QALYs) and disability-adjusted life years (DALYs, see Chap. 14) are both measures of health-adjusted life years (HALYs). Both allow the combined consideration of mortality and morbidity, with the life years being weighted by their health-related quality. QALYs have been mainly developed for use in cost-effectiveness analyses in human health care. They have become one of the most influential tools in human health economics. The metric expresses life expectancy and quality of life in a single value, helping decision-makers compare different treatment options [1].

You might wonder why we have dedicated an entire chapter to the human QALYs. However, there are good reasons why we should not ignore the concept in a book on OR in animal health. The quantification of disease burden similar to the QALYs could be very useful for decision-making, priority setting, and treatment comparisons in animal health care. And the dog health utility index (DHUI) [2] is a preliminary step in creating a QALY-like measure that can be applied when comparing treatments or simply to get an impression of the QoL of the animal.

13.1 Introduction to QALYs

13.1.1 What Is a QALY?

A QALY combines morbidity and mortality in a combined figure, i.e., the quality of life (QoL) of a specific health state and the time lived in this state.

The QoL of a specific health state is expressed as utility, which can take a value between 0 and 1, with 0 being death and 1 perfect health. Accordingly, a utility of 0.5 represents a QoL being assessed as half as good as perfect QoL. In order to finally calculate the QALY, the utility needs to be multiplied with the time being in that health state. Box 13.1 further illustrates the concept.

Box 13.1 One QALY Represents

- 1 year in perfect health: 1×1
- 2 years in a health state being rated half as good as perfect health: 2×0.5
- 4 years in a health state being rated 25% of perfect health: 4×0.25

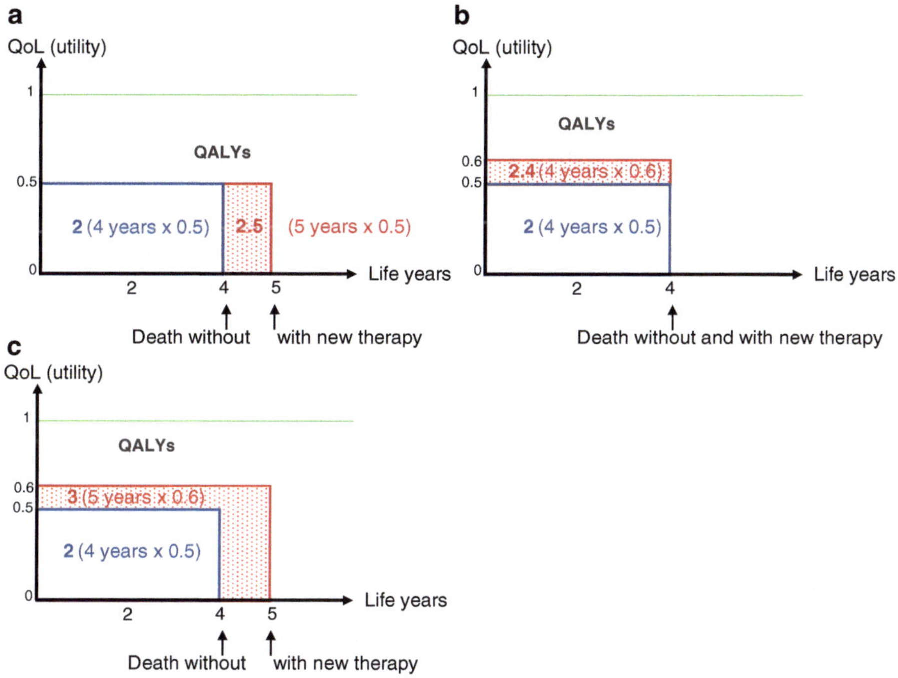

Fig. 13.1 (**a**) Simplified graphical depiction of QALYs gained with a therapy that increases life time without having an impact on QoL. In the given example, the patient gains 0.5 QALYs more with the new therapy. (**b**) Simplified graphical depiction of QALYs gained with a new therapy that increases QoL but does not change life expectancy. In this example, the patient gains 0.4 additional QALYs. (**c**) Simplified graphical depiction of QALYs gained with a new therapy that increases QoL and life expectancy, resulting in one additional QALY in the illustrated example

QALYs are mainly used to compare different health interventions in terms of their impact on life time and QoL. Figure 13.1a–c illustrates how additional QALYs can be gained with a new health intervention compared to current standard, the latter being no treatment or the currently recommended treatment. These illustrations are rather theoretically, as a constant QoL followed by a sudden death is often not a realistic scenario. However, they are intended to illustrate the basic concept, whereas in Box 13.2 a more realistic scenario with two therapy options is displayed.

Box 13.2 The QALY-Concept

Here we show fictive, but more realistic courses of a disease with two treatment options:

- We assume a disease which leads to a progressive decrease of QoL, followed by death.
- A new and aggressive treatment firstly results in a short decrease of QoL after onset of therapy, followed by an increase in QoL. Afterward, QoL is also subsequently decreasing, but remains higher compared to the standard treatment at the defined time points and death occurs later.

Fictive scenario of the evaluation of the course of a disease in animals on standard therapy (displayed in Grey) and those receiving a new therapy (displayed as red line).
The lower QoL after onset of the new therapy compared with standard therapy is displayed by red dots on Grey basis, whereas the higher QoL during the following course of disease is displayed by red dots on white basis.

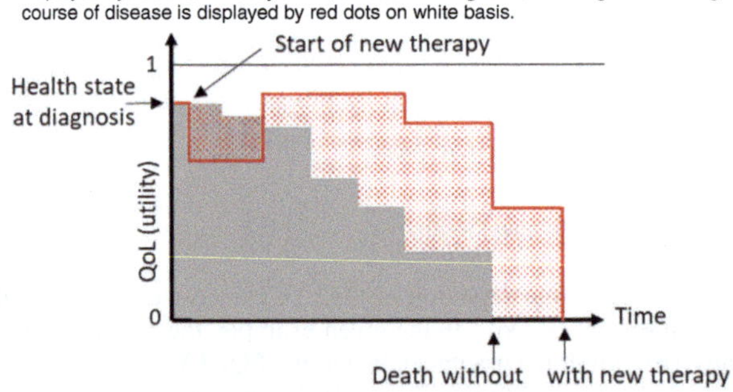

In such cases, QALYs gained with and without new therapy must be calculated for each health state and the time the patients spend in it, being summed up in the end. The QALYs additionally gained with the new therapy correspond to the difference of QALYs gained with and without the new therapy.

13.1.2 Where Do the Utilities Come From?

In human health care, specifically designed index instruments, such as the EuroQol 5-dimension (EQ-5D), health utility index (HUI), and short form 6 dimensions (SF-6D), have been developed which provide utilities for different health states. One of these index instruments has also been preliminarily adapted for use in dogs, the dog health utility index (DHUI) [2]. These instruments have been described in detail in Chap. 12.

It should be noted here that the utilities for use in QALYs are based on health states rather than diseases. The health states are defined by the dimensions included in the index instrument and can be the result of different diseases. We refer to Chap.

12 for a more detailed explanation. In short, the patient fills in the questionnaire and the utilities will be generated according to a priori assessment of the corresponding health state, done by members of the population.

13.1.3 What to Do with a QALY?

A final utility score, quantifying the QoL of an animal at a certain time point, can be used by itself for treatment decision. The author who developed the DHUI proposed an interpretation of the utility score as outlined in Table 13.1 [2]. It must be noted that the scale of the DHUI ranged from 0 to 10 rather than 0 to 1 as common in human index instruments. Accordingly, a score of 5 is equivalent to 0.5 in the human QALY concept.

However, as already mentioned, the QALY concept had been originally developed for use in cost-effectiveness analyses, which are then often referred to as cost-utility analysis, providing the groundwork for decisions on health interventions in human health care when resources are limited.

The calculations are identical to those explained in detail in Chap. 10 (Cost-Effectiveness Analysis). In short, the final outcome of a cost-effectiveness analysis is the incremental cost-effectiveness ratio (ICER), which can represent the cost per life year gained with a new therapy compared to standard therapy. In cost-utility analyses, the ICER represents the cost per additional QALY gained with a new health intervention. An example calculation in Box 13.4 illustrates the concept.

However, the concept is not without criticism. Among others, the often cited phrase "A QALY is a QALY is a QALY" summarizes a main point of criticism, i.e., that all QALYs are considered equal, regardless of the patient and accompanying situation [3]. However, in times of limited resources, decisions might be needed and the QALY-concept provides a well-established tool to support decision-making.

Accordingly, in many countries, cost per QALY gained is the decisive factor, if a new health intervention will be recommended and reimbursed by the payers, i.e., the health system or insurances. As new therapies are often more expensive than current standard treatment, such calculations can be supportive if not decisive.

The threshold, for which new therapies are assessed as acceptable in human medicine differs between countries. In a recent study, the thresholds per QALY gained with a new intervention to be assessed acceptable by authorities varied between USD 87 (Democratic Republic of the Congo), USD 9329 (Argentina), USD 37,952 (UK), and USD 95,958 (USA) [4].

Table 13.1 Proposed interpretation of the QoL quantified with the DHUI [2]

Final QoL score	Proposed interpretation
0–3	Very poor QoL, euthanizing the dog may be proposed
3–5	Very low QoL, improvements must be made directly
5–6	Low QoL, improvement is strongly recommended
6–8	Acceptable QoL
8–10	Good to ideal QoL

Box 13.3 Example of a Cost-Utility Analysis

We adapted this example from "Health economics for non-economists", a book written by the well-known health economist Lieven Annemans [5].

A Markov model was used for the evaluation of two treatment strategies for breast cancer. (We refer here to Chap. 10 which descibes in detail the structure of Markov models as well as the calculation of the incremental cost-effectiveness ratio).

- Therapy costs:
  - Strategy A: € 30,000
  - Strategy B: € 50,000
- The model considers four health states after therapy:
  State 1 No further progression, stable condition without relapse
  State 2 Local relapse (no metastasis)
  State 3 Metastasis
  State 4 Death
- The two strategies (A and B) have different transition probabilities, i.e., probabilities to move into the next (worse) health state and each health state is associated with different costs and utilities as summarized in the following table (adapted from Table 3.7 of [5])

	Cost per 6 months	Utility
State 1	€ 1000	0.8
State 2	€ 5000	0.65
State 3	€ 20,000	0.5
State 4	€ 0	0

- The Markov model calculated the following results:
  - Total costs and QALYs over 10 years:

	Strategy A	Strategy B
Total costs over 10 years	€ 85,090	€ 89,416
QALYs	5.6255	6.3307

  - Incremental cost-effectiveness ratio (ICER):
    (€ 89,416–€ 85,090)/(6.3307–5.6255)
    = € 4327/0.7052
    = *€ 6134.50 per additional QALY gained with Strategy B*
    (Negligible deviations are due to rounding.)

(Example adapted from: Lieven Annemans "Health economics for non-economists" [5])

13.2 Adapting the Concept to Animals

The QALY-concept could offer advantages in veterinary medicine, especially in companion animals. The option to easily define QoL might be helpful for decision-making, e.g., when euthanasia is an option. Additionally, the option to compare costs in relation to the benefit (i.e. life expectancy and QoL in that time) could be supportive for treatment decisions.

A Dutch study performed an important first step: The author adapted the human heath utility index (HUI) for use in dogs. The so-called dog health utility index (DHUI) has been decribed in detail in Chap. 12 of this book. As an example for the use of the DHUI, the authors applied it to dogs with degenerative joint disease, finally comparing three different treatment opti6 ons in terms of QoL and costs. The approach is described in detail in Box 13.4 [2].

Box 13.4 Pesie (2012) Compared Three Treatment Options of Degenerative Joint Disease in Dogs, Following the General Approach of the QALY-Concept [2]

The author used the hypothetical case of an 8-year-old dog, weighing 30 kg which suffers from severe degenerative joint disease in both hind legs.

- Three treatments were compared, with the QoL (utility scores) being estimated with the DHUI:
  - Surgery has a chance of success of 70%, during the 2-months treatment the utility score is 3.5 (out of 10), after successful surgery, the QoL is estimated at 8 (out of 10).
  - Medicines, which have a chance of success of 95%, need to be given continuously and result in a QoL of 6.5 (out of 10).
  - No treatment, which is assigned a utility score of 4.48 (out of 10).

Example calculation for medicinal treatment:

• 95% success: 0.95*6.5	= 6.175
• 5 % failure: 0.05*4.48	= 0.224
Total QoL score:	6.399

(For the calculations of surgery and no treatment we refer to the original article)

- The costs of the three treatments have been estimated as follows:
  - Surgery: € 3000
  - Medicines: € 0.50 per day
  - No treatment: no costs
- Finally, the author calculated the increase of QoL and costs compared to no treatment, if the dog lives another 2 years:
  - Surgery: € 3000 for an increase of 2.175 in QoL
  - Medicines: € 365 for an increase of 1.919 in QoL
- The author concluded that the medicinal therapy is the most beneficial in terms of QoL and costs in this hypothetical case.

From: Pesie, 2012 [2]

Take-Home Messages

- Quality-adjusted life years (QALYs) combine morbidity and mortality into a single measure by multiplying the time spent in a health state by the quality of life associated with that state.
- The QoL is expressed as a value between 0 (death) and 1 (perfect health) which is often called utility.
- QALYs have been mainly developed for use in cost-effectiveness analyses in human health care, which are then called cost-utility analyses. The outcomes help decision-makers compare different treatment options.
- Although not being used in veterinary practice yet, the concept could also be very useful for decision-making, priority setting, and treatment comparisons in animal health care.
- The preliminary development of an index instrument for use in dogs that defines utilities can be regarded as first step.

References

1. Gold MR, Stevenson D, Fryback DG (2002) HALYs and QALYs and DALYs, Oh My: similarities and differences in summary measures of population health. Annu Rev Public Health 23:115–134
2. Pesie S (2012) Quantification of animal disease burden; exploring the possibilities of a dog-health utility index. Msc Thesis Wageningen University. https://library.wur.nl/WebQuery/theses/2016054. Assessed 01 Jul 2025
3. Pettitt DA, Raza S, Naughton B, Roscoe A, Ramakrishnan A, Ali A et al (2016) The limitations of QALY: a literature review. J Stem Cell Res Ther 6(4):1000334
4. Pichon-Riviere A, Drummond M, Palacios A, Garcia-Marti S, Augustovski F (2023) Determining the efficiency path to universal health coverage: cost-effectiveness thresholds for 174 countries based on growth in life expectancy and health expenditures. Lancet Glob Health 11:e833–e842
5. Annemans L (2018) Health economics for non-economics. Pelckmans Pro, Kalmthout

Disability-Adjusted Life Year (DALY) 14

Abstract

Disability-adjusted life years (DALYs) represent the number of healthy life years lost due to disease. They are calculated by combining the years of life lost from premature mortality with the years lived with disability, weighted by a disease-specific severity factor. In this sense, DALYs can be considered the opposite of quality-adjusted life years (QALYs): while QALYs should be maximized for better health, DALYs should be minimized to reduce the impact of disease. Although DALYs were originally developed to evaluate human diseases and guide public health decisions, they have also been adapted for use in animals. The zoonosis DALY (zDALY) expands the human DALY concept to account for the effect of zoonotic diseases in animals. The welfare-adjusted life year (WALY) applies DALY principles to assess welfare loss in veterinary settings. WALYs represent a powerful tool to evaluate welfare compromise and disease impacts in companion and production animals, with wide-ranging potential applications in veterinary health care.

Keywords

Health-adjusted life year · Disability-adjusted life years · DALY · Zoonosis disability-adjusted life years · zDALY · Welfare-adjusted life years · WALY · Impaired welfare weights · Disability weights · Animal loss equivalent

Together with the quality-adjusted life years (QALYs), which were the topic of Chap. 13, the disability-adjusted life years (DALYs) belong to the group of health-adjusted life years (HALYs). These measures allow the combined consideration of mortality and morbidity. While QALYs were mainly developed for use in health economic analyses, the DALYs have been developed by the World Bank and World

B. Poulsen Nautrup, *Outcomes Research in Animal Health Care*,
https://doi.org/10.1007/978-3-032-12587-3_14

Health Organization as a tool to quantify the burden of human diseases. DALYs are commonly used in human public health to help identify disease priorities, especially in countries with limited resources [1]. They have often been used to estimate the burden of zoonotic diseases on humans, thereby identifying the most importance disease to control through intervention in animals that transmit the disease.

The metric has been recently adapted to address the economic impact of zoonotic diseases on animals, being called the zoonosis disability-adjusted life year (zDALY). In addition, the welfare-adjusted life years (WALYs) were introduced for use in animals, evaluating the welfare burden of animal diseases similarly to the DALY-concept in humans.

The three concepts will be outlined in the following sections and a table summarizing their key aspects and differences can be found in Box 14.3.

14.1 DALYs

14.1.1 What Characterizes a DALY?

A DALY reflects the total number of healthy life years lost due to a disease. It is calculated by adding:

- *Years of life lost* due to premature death.
- *Years lived with disability*, adjusted by a weight that represents the severity of the condition.

In this sense, a DALY is like the inverse of a QALY. While QALYs are "good years" of life that you want to maximize, DALYs are "lost years" of good health that you aim to minimize. There are two additional key features which distinguish DALYs from QALYs:

- The DALY uses a standard life-expectancy and the life years lost are calculated as the difference between expected and actual life expectancy
- The weighting of the disabilities in DALYs, i.e., the valuation of the health impairments, is tied to diseases or symptoms rather than to generic, descriptive health states. The disability adjustments are expressed on a scale between 0 (perfect health) and 1 (worst imaginable health state), whereas in QALYs, a score of 1 represents perfect QoL and 0 corresponds to death [1].

14.1.2 How Are DALYs Calculated?

DALYs are calculated by adding the number of life years lost due to premature mortality and the number of years lived with disability, adjusted for the impact of disease. The disability weights correspond to the impairment a disease poses on the patient. As mentioned above, the disability adjustments are expressed on a scale between 0 (perfect health) and 1 (worst imaginable health state). Accordingly, higher figures correspond to more severe diseases, having a greater impact on the patient.

A single DALY corresponds to losing one year of life in perfect health. Alternatively, it can reflect living two years with a disease that has a disability weight of 0.5. We will further illustrate the calculation in Box 14.1, using a simplified example.

Box 14.1: The Calculation of DALYs
We assume the following simplified example of a dog with an average life expectancy of 12 years:

- At the age of 6 years, the dog develops diabetes
- The disability weight of diabetes is estimated at 0.3
- The dog dies at age of 10 (2 years before the expected lifespan of 12 years)

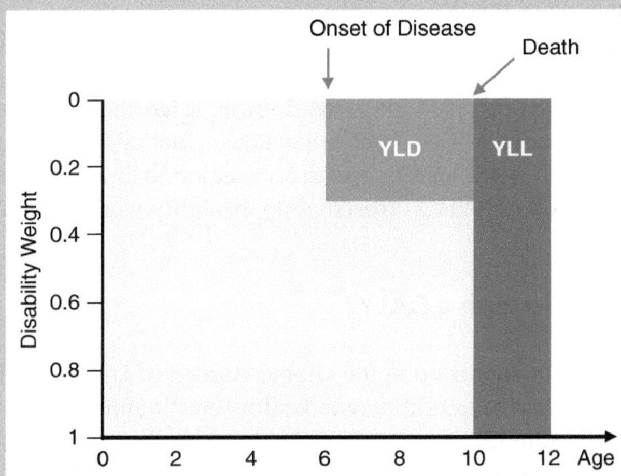

Calculation:

- Years Lived with Disability (YLD): 4 years * 0.3 = 1.2 years
- Years of Life Lost (YLL): 2 years * 1 = 2 years
- Total DALYs: 3.2 years

So, diabetes in this dog accounted for a total loss of 3.2 healthy life years.

In contrast to QALYs, which are calculated for different health states throughout the disease, the disability weights considered in DALYs are mostly kept constant throughout the patient's residual life expectancy or disease duration.

14.1.3 Where Do the Disability Weights Come From?

In human medicine, disability weights are commonly determined by health professionals or by members of the entire population. In the study introducing the WALY for dogs, the so-called impaired welfare weights were defined by veterinarians [2].

▶ Important Note:
The selection of the group of people that define the weights can have a relevant impact, as they might value or rank the severity of conditions in different ways. For example, farmers or animal owners might weight the diseases differently from veterinarians.

There are two different approaches to define the disability or impaired welfare weights of a specific disease:

- A generic approach: Here welfare impediments are defined, which can apply to different diseases. For example, disability weights that have been defined for mild, moderate, and severe heart failure, can be used for different heart diseases, such as mitral valve disease or dilated cardiomyopathy. This approach was used for the estimation of the WALYs [2].
- A disease-specific approach: When using this approach, the disability weights are defined for a specific disease, e.g., mammary tumor in dogs. Although this approach allows the precise link to the disease, it has the disadvantage of mentioning the disease. This "label" can impact the valuation, as mentioning the term "tumor or cancer" might lead to a worse valuation than a disability weight that would be defined if only the corresponding disability would be valuated.

14.1.4 What to Do with a DALY?

The DALY is a core metric used in the Global Burden of Disease (GBD) program, which is a large-scale research in human health care. It aims to quantify and compare health losses from diseases, injuries, and risk factors worldwide. These estimates are regularly updated and help policymakers, researchers, and public-health experts to pinpoint which diseases have the greatest overall impact and to decide how to allocate resources to reduce the highest burdens.

However, when deciding on a program intended to control a disease, also costs need to be considered. In the end, total costs of the program can be expressed in relation to the DALYs averted, i.e., the cost per DALY averted. Accordingly, this approach parallels the "cost per QALY gained" in classical health economics, a concept that has been outlined in the preceding Chap. 13.

A study evaluated thresholds for a program to be regarded as cost-effective in countries with different income levels. On average, the acceptable cost per DALY averted was USD 998, USD 6522, USD 23,782, and USD 69,499 in low-, medium-, high-, and very-high-income countries, respectively [3]. The values can be regarded as cost-effectiveness thresholds applied in different countries.

14.1.5 What Are the Main Drawbacks of DALYs?

Disability weights in DALYs cannot take into account comorbidities, as DALY weights are not designed to consider different illnesses within the same patient. Similarly, side effects of a therapy cannot be captured within the DALY framework.

For instance, if a dog is treated for osteoarthritis with medication that causes gastrointestinal issues, DALYs might not capture the overall decrease in well-being from these combined effects.

14.2 The zoonosis DALY (zDALY)

The DALY framework has been extended to the "zoonosis DALY" (zDALY) by adding an additional component that reflects the economic impact of the disease on the animal: the animal loss equivalent (ALE). The ALE aims to capture the economic losses an animal owner faces if the animal becomes ill or dies, corresponding to the time required for an animal owner to recoup the losses caused by the illness [4].

The zDALY is calculated as follows:

$$\text{zDALY} = \text{life years lost} + \text{life years lived with disability} + \text{animal loss equivalent}$$

Because a single animal's illness or death might be far more serious for a small-scale farmer with low income than for a large commercial operation in a wealthier region, the ALE is adjusted to reflect local per capita income. Therefore, the same losses result in much lower ALEs in high-income countries than in low-income countries, as the ALE refers to the days of work necessary to recoup the losses.

The concept is illustrated in Box 14.2.

Box 14.2: The Animal Loss Equivalent (ALE)

Torgerson et al. (2018) explained the basis of the ALE, using the following scenario:

- Considering differences in productivity in different production systems, the loss of a cow due to disease is estimated to be:
  - For a subsistence farmer in sub-Saharan Africa, USD 500
  - For a farmer from an industrialized nation, USD 1000
- Considering differences in annual income in different countries
  - USD 1000 for the subsistence farmer in sub-Saharan Africa
  - USD 40,000 for the farmer in an industrialized nation
- The working time required to recover the costs is
  - 6 months for the subsistence farmer in sub-Saharan Africa
  - 1.3 weeks for the farmer in an industrialized nation

The same approach can also be applied to production losses, such as milk losses. By including the ALE, zDALYs highlight how severely smallholders in low-income countries might be affected by losses due to animal diseases and policymakers can better recognize and address the broader economic impact of zoonotic diseases [4].

14.3 Welfare-Adjusted Life Year (WALY)

Finally, we come to the adaptation of the DALY concept to animals, the welfare-adjusted life years (WALYs). The WALYs combine the welfare compromise and premature death component due to a specific animal disease. The calculation is similar to that of a DALY, adding the life years lost and years lived with impaired welfare. The concept has been first applied to dog diseases. The authors of the study estimated WALYs for 10 common canine diseases [2], which have been summarized in Table 14.1.

These figures represent the healthy life years lost due to each disease. Accordingly, higher WALYs indicate a greater burden, reflecting both welfare compromise and reduced lifespan. The authors concluded that WALYs could become a powerful metric to summarize welfare compromise and disease impact of individual conditions in companion animals and potentially also in livestock [2]. In accordance with these perceptions, Steeneveld et al. (2024) proposed the WALY-concept to quantify the noneconomic burdens of disease and reproductive inefficiency in dairy cows. The authors recommended using a realistic longevity estimate for dairy cows under production conditions, rather than relying on the life expectancy of animals outside of production systems. Furthermore, they emphasized that baseline welfare levels may vary between different production systems, being lower in tiestall barns than in a freestall barns or grazing systems [5].

Table 14.1 WALYs estimated by Teng et al. (2018) for 10 canine diseases

Disease	Weighted WALYs
Mitral valve disease	2.54 (1.21–4.61)
Dilated cardiomyopathy	4.27 (3.47–5.13)
Chronic kidney disease	2.55 (1.08–5.51)
Diabetes mellitus	3.02 (1.63–5.12)
Atopic dermatitis	9.73 (7.17–11.8)
Splenic hemangiosarcoma	2.93 (1.92–4.04)
Appendicular osteosarcoma	4.29 (2.52–6.55)
Cranial cruciate ligament disease	3.47 (2.39–4.58)
Thoracolumbar intervertebral disc disease	2.69 (1.14–3.75)
Cervical spondylomyelopathy	4.61 (3.40–6.00)

Adapted from Table 7 of [2]

These values represent the average loss of healthy life years attributable to each disease. Numbers in parentheses indicate the 95% uncertainty interval

Box 14.3: Comparison of the Three Metrics: DALY, zDALY, and WALY

Metric	Purpose	Calculation and components	Main uses
DALY (Disability-Adjusted Life Year)	Traditional human health metric Quantifies the overall burden of disease in humans	**DALY = YLL + YLD** **YLL**: Years of Life Lost due to premature death. **YLD**: Years Lived with Disability, weighted by disease severity	Public health planning and priority-setting at population/national level Evaluating cost-effectiveness of interventions by examining cost per DALY averted
zDALY (zoonosis DALY)	Designed for zoonoses Extends the DALY concept to include the economic impact of zoonotic diseases on animals	**zDALY = YLL + YLD + ALE** **YLL**: Years of Life Lost due to premature death. **YLD**: Years Lived with Disability, weighted by disease severity **ALE**: Animal Loss Equivalent, quantifies the economic loss incurred due to an animal's illness/death	Assessing burden of zoonotic diseases, especially when animal health losses are economically critical
WALY (Welfare-Adjusted Life Year)	Adapts the DALY-methodology to animals, combining the welfare impairment and premature death in animals	**WALY = YLL + YLIW** **YLL**: Years of Life Lost due to premature death. **YLIW**: Years Lived with Impaired Welfare	Quantifying the welfare impact of diseases in companion or production animals Guiding veterinary decision-making where health and well-being (rather than only economics) drive interventions

Take-Home Messages

- Disability-adjusted life years combine the number of life years lost due to premature mortality and the number of years lived with disability, adjusted for the impact of disease on the patient.
- When evaluating the public health burden of zoonoses, the DALY is a commonly used and appropriate metric.
- The development of the zDALY allows the additional consideration of the impact of zoonoses on the animals.
- The WALY-concept, an adaptation of the DALY-concept for use in animals, allows the quantification of the welfare burden of diseases on affected animals, offering many potential future applications.

References

1. Gold MR, Stevenson D, Fryback DG (2002) HALYs and QALYs and DALYs, oh my: similarities and differences in summary measures of population health. Annu Rev Public Health 23:115–134
2. Teng KTY, Devleesschauwer B, Maertens De Noordhout C, Bennett P, McGreevy PD, Chiu PY et al (2018) Welfare-Adjusted Life Years (WALY): a novel metric of animal welfare that combines the impacts of impaired welfare and abbreviated lifespan. PLoS ONE 13(9):e0202580
3. Daroudi R, Akbari Sari A, Nahvijou A, Faramarzi A (2021) Cost per DALY averted in low, middle- and high-income countries: evidence from the global burden of disease study to estimate the cost-effectiveness thresholds. Cost Eff Resour Alloc 19:7
4. Torgerson PR, Rüegg S, Devleesschauwer B, Abela-Ridder B, Havelaar AH, Shaw APM et al (2018) zDALY: An adjusted indicator to estimate the burden of zoonotic diseases. One Health 5:40–45
5. Steeneveld W, Van Den Borne BHP, Kok A, Rodenburg TB, Hogeveen H (2024) Invited review: quantifying multiple burdens of dairy cattle production diseases and reproductive inefficiency – current knowledge and proposed metrics. J Dairy Sci 107:8765–8795

Glossary

Absorbing state A health state in health economic models that, once entered, cannot be left; with death being a common example.

Adherence Following the treatment or management recommendations of a health professional as part of an active, informed partnership, rather than through passive obedience.

Animal Health Loss Envelope (AHLE) A Global Burden of Animal Diseases (GBADs) metric that shows the total financial costs of an animal disease at farm level. It sums the value of production lost because animals perform below their disease-free potential and the expenditures for disease control and compares this to a disease-free ideal.

Animal Loss Equivalent (ALE) It shows how much human work time would be needed to make up for the money lost when an animal gets sick or dies. It adjusts for local wage levels, helping compare the impact of animal disease across different countries.

Animal welfare The term is often used interchangeably with "quality of life." When applied to livestock, however, it is often based on the "Five Freedoms," evaluating whether basic needs of the animals, such as nutrition, comfort, health, normal behavior, and freedom from fear and distress, are met.

Benefit-Cost Ratio (BCR) A measure of the economic return on investment: the discounted benefits of an intervention are divided by its total discounted costs. A BCR above 1.0 indicates the intervention returns more money than it costs.

Bias In clinical studies, bias refers to systematic errors that arise when factors such as participant selection (selection bias), data measurement (information bias), or outcome reporting (publication bias) are not adequately addressed, reducing the validity and generalizability of findings.

Big data Extremely large and complex digital datasets that exceed the capacity of traditional data-management tools to capture, store, and analyze. In animal health care, big data can originate from electronic medical records, on-farm sensors and wearables, and production or movement logs, and it is often interrogated with advanced analytics and machine learning.

Binary data Data with only two possible outcomes, typically coded as 0 and 1. In outcomes research, binary data typically represent the presence or absence

B. Poulsen Nautrup, *Outcomes Research in Animal Health Care*,
https://doi.org/10.1007/978-3-032-12587-3

of an event, for example, treatment success vs. failure or disease occurrence vs. non-occurrence.

Bioequivalence A condition in which two pharmaceutical products release their active ingredient at the same rate and extent, producing equivalent effects in the body.

Bottom-up (micro-) costing A detailed costing approach that identifies every individual resource item and multiplies it by its unit price, e.g., number of veterinary consultations multiplied by price per consultation. It yields high precision but requires extensive data collection.

Burden of disease study This study type quantifies the impact of diseases on animal populations by considering their prevalence or incidence, along with outcomes such as morbidity, mortality, and productivity loss. The studies may also account for the effects of treatments or preventive measures, altogether helping to prioritize interventions and inform animal health policy and resource allocation.

Case-Control Study A retrospective design that compares animals that have the outcome of interest (cases) with similar animals that do not (controls), then looks back to assess previous exposure. Because the size of the source population is unknown, associations are commonly expressed as odds ratios that do not allow the quantification of absolute risk between groups.

Cluster Randomized Study Design A design frequently used in livestock studies where whole pens, herds, or flocks are randomly assigned to treatment and control groups. This reflects husbandry systems where individual treatment is impractical or where treating some animals could influence outcomes in others within the same group.

Comorbidity The presence of two or more diseases or health conditions in the same animal at the same time.

Compliance The extent to which an animal caretaker follows treatment regimens (e.g., dosing schedules), management recommendations, laws, regulations, or guidelines. Non-compliance might bear the risk of treatment failure, antimicrobial resistance, and reduced animal welfare or productivity.

Confounding Bias This type of bias arises when the relationship between an exposure and an outcome is distorted by a third variable (a confounder) that is associated with both. For example, if animals receiving a new treatment are also cared for by more attentive caretakers, health improvements may reflect better management rather than the treatment effect.

Continuous data Numerical data that can take any value within a given range, allowing for fractional or decimal values. In outcomes research, they represent variables like blood sugar, weight gain, or quality-of-life scores.

Cost-benefit analysis (CBA) An economic evaluation in which all effects and costs of a health or management intervention are expressed in monetary units and compared. It assesses whether the total benefits of the intervention exceed its total costs, often to support decision-making in livestock systems.

Cost-Effectiveness Analysis (CEA) A health-economic method that compares the costs of interventions with their physiological or welfare outcomes, without converting those outcomes into monetary terms. It is especially useful in animal health when monetizing outcomes, such as quality of life gains in companion animals, is difficult or inappropriate.

Cost-Effectiveness Plane A two-dimensional graph where the x-axis shows incremental effectiveness and the y-axis shows incremental costs between two health interventions. The four quadrants quickly reveal whether a new option is more or less costly and more or less effective.

Cost-minimization analysis A type of economic study that compares only the costs of interventions, assuming that their effectiveness is equal. It should only be used when equal effectiveness has been clearly demonstrated.

Cost of disease study An economic evaluation that estimates the monetary losses associated with a specific disease, either on a per-case basis or by factoring in its frequency (incidence or prevalence) in the population. These studies are typically narrower in scope than burden of disease studies, focusing on direct financial impacts rather than the broader impact on the animal population.

Cost-utility analysis (CUA) A type of cost-effectiveness analysis that uses the quality-adjusted life year (QALY) as the outcome measure. Results are expressed as the cost per additional QALY gained compared to another treatment, making it a preferred approach in human healthcare to demonstrate value for money and guide resource allocation across different conditions.

Cross-Over Design A controlled trial in which each animal receives all treatments in a pre-defined order, separated by a washout period, allowing the animal to serve as its own control. Investigators must assess and, if needed, adjust for carry-over effects that may occur when treatments are applied sequentially.

Decision Tree A simple, intuitive model used to compare treatment options in short-term healthcare scenarios. Each branch of the tree represents possible outcomes, their probabilities, and associated costs and benefits; by combining these, the model estimates the average cost and benefit of each option.

Delta profit (Δ profit) A simple measure of how much the profit changes after a management decision. The change in profit is calculated as gains (extra income and saved costs) minus losses (new costs and lost income). As the measure does not account for the timing of money, it is mainly used for simple, short-term farm-level interventions.

Deterministic Sensitivity Analysis A method that systematically varies model input parameters over a predefined range to examine how they affect the results. Parameters are changed one at a time or in combination to identify those with the greatest influence. Key types include one-way, two-way, and multi-way sensitivity analyses.

Disability weight A value between 0 (perfect animal health) and 1 (worst imaginable health state) that quantifies how much a condition or disease impairs quality of life. It is a key part of calculating the disability-adjusted life year (DALY).

Disability-Adjusted Life Year (DALY) A human-health metric that combines years of life lost due to premature death with years lived with disability, reflecting total health loss from disease. The impact of disability is quantified using a disability weight specific to each disease or condition. DALYs are widely used in burden of disease studies and zoonosis control programs, and they have inspired a similar composite measure in animal health economics, the welfare-adjusted life year (WALY).

Discounting An adjustment that converts future costs and benefits into present-day values, based on the principle that resources are generally valued higher now than in the future. A discount rate is applied in analyses spanning multiple years to reflect this time preference.

Disease-specific questionnaire A quality of life survey tailored to a single condition (e.g., canine osteoarthritis). It can detect small changes in affected animals, for instance due to treatment, but may miss the effect of comorbidities or side effects.

Dog Health Utility Index (DHUI) An early tool for converting canine quality of life into a single "utility" score, based on factors such as pain, mobility, mental state, and cognition. It represents a preliminary attempt to develop a dog-specific equivalent of the human QALY.

Dominant Strategy An intervention that is both less costly and more effective than the alternative, making it the preferred choice in cost-effectiveness analysis.

Effect size A numerical measure (such as a mean difference or risk ratio) that quantifies how much better or worse one intervention performs compared to another. In meta-analyses, an effect size is calculated for each included study, and these are then combined to produce a summary estimate of the average effect across all studies.

Effectiveness The outcome achieved under real-world conditions, where different breeds or factors like compliance, comorbidities, and management practices may vary. It reflects the actual benefit of an intervention in everyday settings rather than the efficacy measured in tightly controlled experimental trials.

Efficacy The outcome measured under tightly controlled clinical-trial conditions with strict patient management and intensive monitoring. The reported efficacy often exceeds the effectiveness observed in routine practice.

Equivalence trial A study designed to determine whether two interventions produce outcomes that are statistically and clinically similar within a pre-specified margin.

Eradication program A coordinated effort to completely eliminate a disease from a defined population or region, often involving testing, culling, vaccination, and movement controls. True eradication means reducing disease incidence to zero in the target area and maintaining that status.

Evidence pyramid A visual hierarchy of study designs ranked by the strength of their evidence. At the base are expert opinions and case reports; higher up are cohort studies and randomized controlled trials, with meta-analyses at the top, representing the most reliable evidence.

External validity The extent to which study findings can be generalized to the broader animal population or typical daily practice settings. Features of experimental clinical trials, such as strict inclusion criteria, intensive monitoring, and ideal compliance, may reduce external validity by limiting the transferability of results to real-world conditions.

Externalities Costs or benefits that affect others who are not directly involved in, or paying for an intervention. For example, vaccinating one herd may reduce disease spread to neighboring farms, providing a benefit to others at no cost to them.

Five Freedoms A well-established animal welfare framework that outlines five essential conditions: freedom from hunger and thirst, freedom from discomfort, freedom from pain, injury, or disease, freedom from fear and distress, and the freedom to express normal behavior. These principles serve as the foundation for many animal welfare assessment tools.

Fixed-effect model In meta-analysis, this model assumes that all studies estimate the same underlying true effect and that any observed differences between study results are solely due to random sampling error. However, when clinical or methodological diversity is anticipated, a random-effects model is generally preferred.

Forest Plot A graphical summary of results from multiple studies, commonly used in meta-analyses. It displays the effect estimates and confidence intervals for each study, along with the overall combined effect, allowing for easy comparison of consistency and relative weight across studies.

Funnel plot A scatterplot used in meta-analysis to assess publication bias by plotting study precision against effect size. In the absence of bias, the plot typically forms a symmetrical funnel shape. Asymmetry may suggest that smaller studies with non-significant or unfavorable results are under-represented, possibly due to selective publication or reporting.

Generic questionnaire A quality of life instrument developed for use across different diseases or health conditions within a specific animal species. Although it may be less sensitive to particular clinical issues, it allows for comparison between individuals or groups with varying health statuses or comorbidities.

Global Burden of Animal Diseases (GBADs) program An international research partnership that builds standardized data sets and metrics to quantify the economic, social, and environmental impacts of livestock and aquaculture diseases worldwide. By measuring production losses, health-care expenditures, and related societal costs, GBADs provides evidence to guide policy decisions and investment in animal-health systems.

Health Economics (HE) The branch of economics that studies how scarce resources (e.g. money, staff, time) can be allocated efficiently to improve health. It compares the costs and health outcomes of different interventions (like drugs, programs, or policies) to support decision-making.

Health Economics and Outcomes Research (HEOR) The term HEOR is widely used in human health care, recognizing the close ties between health economics and outcomes research. The field combines health economics with the measurement of real-world clinical, quality-of-life, and productivity outcomes. It aims to evaluate not just how much an intervention costs, but what value it provides, thereby helping veterinarians, policymakers, and producers make informed decisions by comparing the benefits and costs of different strategies under real-world conditions.

Heterogeneity In meta-analysis, heterogeneity refers to variation among study results beyond random error, driven by differences in design, populations, interventions, or outcome measures. Recognizing heterogeneity is essential for determining whether studies can be meaningfully combined and how to interpret the overall result.

Incidence The number of new cases of a disease occurring in a population over a defined period of time. The incidence rate reflects the rate at which animals are becoming newly affected and is essential for understanding disease dynamics and planning control measures.

Inconsistency In network meta-analysis, inconsistency occurs when the effect estimate from head-to-head studies differs significantly from the estimate derived indirectly through the evidence network, indicating possible problems with study comparability or model assumptions.

Incremental Cost-Effectiveness Ratio (ICER) A summary measure that compares two health interventions by calculating the additional cost required to achieve one extra unit of health benefit, such as the cost per additional life year gained with the intervention of interest. It is computed by dividing the difference in costs by the difference in effects, helping decision-makers assess whether the added benefit of an intervention justifies its extra cost.

Index instrument A type of generic quality of life questionnaire designed to generate utility values, i.e., a numerical weight for a given health state, for use in quality-adjusted life year (QALY) calculations. While originally developed for human health, a first tool has been preliminarily developed for use in veterinary research (the dog health utility index).

Inflation adjustment Updating of historical cost values to reflect current-year prices, using appropriate price indices relevant to the sector. This process ensures that costs from different years are comparable, allowing for consistent and accurate economic evaluations.

Intangible costs These costs refer to non-financial harms, such as pain, fear, emotional distress, or reduced quality of life, caused by diseases, injuries, environmental events, or other adverse situations. While these costs are difficult to express in money terms, they are essential for capturing the full burden of any intervention or event.

Internal rate of return (IRR) A financial metric used in cost–benefit analysis that represents the discount rate at which a project's net present value equals zero. If the IRR exceeds the return of alternative investment options, the project is considered economically attractive.

Internal Validity The extent to which a study accurately shows that the observed effects are caused by the intervention itself, rather than by confounding factors, bias, or other methodological flaws. High internal validity means the results can be confidently attributed to the intervention, thanks to rigorous design features such as randomization, blinding, and control of confounders.

Markov Model A state-transition model used in health economic analysis to simulate how individuals move between defined health states (e.g., healthy, sick, dead) over time. It is especially useful for chronic or recurring conditions, as it can reflect the typical course of a disease and capture long-term costs and outcomes.

Meta-analysis A statistical technique that combines results from multiple comparable studies to produce a precise and reliable estimate of a treatment effect. It helps resolve conflicting findings, enhances statistical power, and is considered one of the highest levels of evidence in research synthesis.

Meta-regression A meta-analytic technique that uses regression techniques to explore how study-level factors (e.g., dosage, study design, or duration) influence treatment effects across studies. It helps explain heterogeneity but requires a sufficient number of studies to produce reliable results.

Monte Carlo Simulation A method used in health economic modeling to assess uncertainty by repeatedly running the model with random values drawn from probability distributions assigned to uncertain parameters (e.g., costs, probabilities, or utilities). This produces a range of possible outcomes and supports probabilistic sensitivity analysis to inform decision-making under uncertainty.

Net present value (NPV) A common outcome in cost-benefit analysis, representing the difference between the total discounted costs of a project and its total discounted benefits. A positive NPV means the intervention earns more than its opportunity cost and thus adds economic value.

Network meta-analysis An extension of meta-analysis that compares multiple treatments by combining direct evidence from head-to-head trials with indirect evidence from studies sharing a common comparator. This method allows estimating the relative effectiveness of treatments, even when they have not been directly compared.

Non-compliance Any deviation from prescribed instructions or guidelines, including missed, delayed, or incorrect doses, failure to follow management or husbandry advice, or disregard for legal or regulatory requirements. It can reduce clinical effectiveness, compromise animal welfare, foster antimicrobial resistance, undermine client trust, and jeopardize farm productivity and public health.

Non-inferiority trial A study designed to show that a new treatment is not worse than an existing treatment by more than a predefined margin, sometimes used when the new option offers other advantages, such as lower costs.

Observational study A non-experimental study in which the investigator observes exposures and outcomes as they naturally occur, without assigning or controlling interventions. Observational research is widely used to assess the real-world use, effectiveness, and safety of interventions in routine clinical practice, but results must be interpreted with careful attention to potential confounding and bias.

Odds ratio A statistic that compares the odds that an event occurs in one group with the odds that the same event occurs in another group. An odds ratio above 1 means the event is more likely in the first group, while a value below 1 means it is less likely. Because odds express the chance of an event relative to its non-occurrence, odds ratios can be less intuitive than risk ratios.

One Health An interdisciplinary approach that recognizes the interconnectedness of human, animal, and environmental health. It promotes collaboration across sectors to address shared challenges like zoonotic diseases, antimicrobial resistance, and food safety.

One-way sensitivity analysis A deterministic method where one input in a model is varied across a plausible range while all others are held constant to assess how much that input affects the result. It helps identify the most influential parameters and is often illustrated using a tornado diagram.

Opportunity costs The benefits lost when a resource such as money, time, labor, or space is used for a particular purpose. Recognizing opportunity costs helps ensure that limited resources are allocated as efficiently as possible.

Partial budgeting A financial tool used at the farm level to evaluate the economic impact of a specific management change by analyzing the costs and benefits that will change. It typically covers a short time frame, so discounting future values is not required.

Persistence The length of time an animal stays on therapy, irrespective of how precisely each dose is taken. Whereas compliance focuses on day-to-day dosing accuracy, persistence tracks whether treatment continues for the full recommended duration.

Perspective The analytic viewpoint adopted in an economic study, e.g., the societal or governmental perspective, or the perspective of the animal owner, farm manager, or veterinarian. The chosen perspective determines which costs and benefits must be counted.

Pharmacokinetics The branch of pharmacology that examines the time course of a drug within the body. It includes the absorption, distribution, metabolism, and excretion of the drug.

Post-Marketing Surveillance Study An observational study conducted after regulatory approval to monitor real-world effectiveness and detect rare or long-term adverse events across diverse settings, including different breeds, ages, husbandry systems, and management practices.

Prevalence The proportion of animals in a defined population that have a specified condition at a given point (point prevalence) or over a defined period (period prevalence).

Probabilistic Sensitivity Analysis (PSA) A method that assigns probability distributions to uncertain model inputs instead of fixed point estimates. The model is then run many times, typically via Monte-Carlo simulation, to generate a range of possible outcomes, helping quantify uncertainty and assess the robustness of the results.

Prospective Cohort Study A forward-looking observational design in which groups of animals with differing exposures or other risk factors are enrolled and followed over time to compare outcome rates. Large, long-running cohorts can quantify absolute and relative risks and uncover exposure-disease associations.

Proxy In the context of quality of life assessment, proxy refers to a person, such as the animal owner, caretaker, or veterinarian, who provides observations or judgments on behalf of the animal, which cannot self-report.

Publication bias A distortion that occurs when studies, especially those with non-significant or negative results, are less likely to be published. This selective reporting can lead to an unrepresentative sample of studies in meta-analyses, exaggerating benefits or underestimating harms.

Quality of Life (QoL) A multidimensional assessment of an animal's overall well-being, integrating both negative and positive physical, psychological, and social experiences as perceived by the animal. Because animals cannot self-report, QoL is typically inferred through behavioral, clinical, and contextual observations.

Quality-Adjusted Life Year (QALY) A widely used measure in human health economics that combines the time a person spends in specific health states with the quality of those states, using utility values ranging from 0 (death) to 1 (perfect health). It allows comparisons across healthcare interventions by capturing both survival and the impact of disease or treatment on quality of life.

Random-effects model A meta-analysis approach that assumes true effect sizes vary across studies due to differences in populations, settings, or methods. It is especially suitable when heterogeneity is expected, as often occurs in animal studies where factors like species, husbandry, or management practices can differ.

Randomized Controlled Trial (RCT) An experimental clinical study in which subjects are randomly assigned to a treatment group and at least one concurrent control group (e.g., placebo or standard care). Randomization reduces baseline differences between groups, allowing for unbiased comparisons and giving RCTs the highest internal validity in the evidence hierarchy of clinical studies.

Regression line A fitted line through data points in a scatterplot, showing the estimated relationship between one variable and another. In meta-regression and similar analyses, it helps illustrate how outcomes change in relation to study factors such as treatment dose or duration, or population characteristics.

Resource use In health-economic analyses, it refers to the physical quantities of goods and services consumed in preventing, diagnosing, or treating a disease, such as clinic visits, drug doses, laboratory tests, procedures, or staff time. When multiplied by unit costs, these quantities allow estimation of the economic burden of a disease or the cost of an intervention.

Retrospective Study An observational study that looks backward in time, when outcomes have already occurred. The investigators use existing records (e.g., clinic logs, herd data, or other databases) to explore associations and capture real-world evidence. Such studies are typically faster and less expensive than prospective ones, though their findings may be limited by the quality and completeness of the available data.

Risk Ratio A measure, also called relative risk, that compares the probability of an outcome in one group (e.g., treatment or exposed) to that in another (e.g., control or unexposed). A risk ratio of 1 indicates no difference in risk; values above or below 1 indicate higher or lower risk in the first group relative to the second.

Scatterplot In probabilistic sensitivity analyses, a scatterplot displays the results of multiple Monte Carlo simulations, with each dot representing a paired cost and effect estimate from a single model run. The resulting cloud of points helps visualize how much results vary and how uncertain the overall conclusion is.

Sensitivity Analysis A set of techniques that tests how uncertainty in model inputs, such as costs or treatment effects, affects the results of a health-economic model and thus the robustness of its conclusions. Key methods include deterministic analysis, which changes one or a few inputs at a time, and probabilistic analysis, which varies all inputs simultaneously according to probability distributions.

Stakeholders All parties affected by or involved in a decision. In animal health care, this may include pet owners, livestock producers, veterinarians, insurers, government bodies, industry groups, or animal welfare organizations.

Standard gamble In the context of health economics, this preference-based method measures how desirable a health state is by asking individuals to choose between living with that state for sure or taking a gamble between perfect health and immediate death. The chance of perfect health is gradually increased or decreased until the person can no longer choose between the two options and this probability of indifference becomes the utility value of the health state.

Stochastic Model A model that considers random variation to reflect how real-life outcomes, such as health results or costs, can differ from patient to patient or over time. Instead of providing just one outcome, it runs many simulations to show a range of possible results. This type of model is often used in health economics to reflect variability and test how reliable the results are under uncertainty.

Subgroup analysis In meta-analysis, a subgroup analysis checks whether the results differ across specific groups of studies or populations, for example, by grouping studies according to quality, publication type, or the setting in which the intervention was delivered. These analyses can reveal important patterns, but they should be planned in advance, as conducting them after seeing the results can lead to misleading or unreliable conclusions.

Surrogate Parameter A laboratory test or biomarker that stands in for a clinical outcome that is harder to measure directly. Examples include using blood-glucose levels as a proxy for long-term diabetes complications, or counting parasite eggs in feces instead of tracking overall productivity. Surrogates allow faster trials but may not fully capture the treatment's full impact on health or performance.

Systematic literature search and review A planned, transparent process for locating, evaluating, and combining all relevant research on a clearly defined question. It follows a written protocol that outlines the search strategy, inclusion and exclusion criteria, quality appraisal, and data synthesis, in order to gather evidence comprehensively, minimize bias, and allow others to reproduce the review.

Time trade-off (TTO) A preference-based technique in which respondents indicate how many years of perfect health they would give up to avoid living longer in a poorer health state. The trade-off involves sacrificing years of healthy life to escape an impaired condition, yielding a numerical value for the desirability of the impaired health state, i.e., the utility.

Top-down costing A costing approach that begins with broad, aggregate expenditure data, such as national or regional budgets, and allocates these totals to specific diseases, interventions, or populations based on proportions or assumptions. It allows for rapid, high-level estimates useful in policy or sector-wide analysis, but may lack the precision needed for detailed, farm-level evaluations.

Tornado Diagram A horizontal bar chart used in one-way sensitivity analysis to show how changes in individual input parameters affect the results of a model. Parameters are ranked from most to least influential, giving the chart its characteristic funnel or "tornado" shape. The wider the bar, the greater that parameter's impact on the outcome, helping identify which inputs have the greatest influence and may need closer attention or refinement.

Transitivity In network meta-analysis, transitivity is the assumption that indirect comparisons between treatments are valid because the included studies are sufficiently similar in key aspects, such as patient populations, interventions, and outcome measures. This similarity, along with the presence of a common comparator, allows researchers to estimate the relative effectiveness of treatments that have not been directly compared in the same study.

Trim-and-fill method A statistical technique used in meta-analysis to detect and adjust for publication bias, which can occur when studies with non-significant or negative results are less likely to be published. The method identifies asymmetry in a funnel plot, "trims" potentially biased studies, imputes missing studies to restore balance, and then recalculates an adjusted overall effect estimate.

Uncertainty In economic evaluations, uncertainty refers to the unavoidable imprecision in model inputs, assumptions, and predictions. It arises from random error, limited data, and real variability in populations or outcomes. Identifying these sources and assessing their influence on results is essential for judging the robustness of a study's conclusions.

Utility A numerical weight that reflects the desirability of a health or welfare state, usually scaled from 0 (death) to 1 (perfect health). Utilities are used to calculate QALYs (quality-adjusted life years) in human health economics and have been adapted to animals; for example, the dog health utility index (DHUI) assigns scores to canine health states to inform clinical and economic decisions.

Welfare-adjusted life year (WALY) As an animal-specific adaptation of the DALY (disability-adjusted life year), the WALY quantifies the total welfare burden of a disease by combining years of life lost due to premature death with years lived in a state of impaired welfare. It is used to assess and compare the burden of different animal diseases.

Willingness-to-pay (WTP) In animal health care, this valuation method estimates how much owners or other stakeholders are willing to pay for a health or welfare gain. It can be used in cost-benefit analyses to help quantify non-market benefits, such as pain reduction in pets or improved welfare in livestock.

Zoonosis A disease that is naturally transmissible between animals and humans, with consequences for animal welfare, human health, and the broader economy. Addressing these diseases calls for a One Health perspective that links veterinary, public-health, and environmental actions.

Zoonosis DALY (zDALY) An extension of the disability-adjusted life year (DALY) that adds an "Animal Loss Equivalent" to capture the economic impact of zoonotic diseases on livestock and companion animals. By combining human health losses with animal-related economic losses in a single measure, it offers a more comprehensive view of the total burden of zoonoses.

Index

B. Poulsen Nautrup, *Outcomes Research in Animal Health Care*,
https://doi.org/10.1007/978-3-032-12587-3

MIX
Papier aus verantwortungsvollen Quellen
Paper from responsible sources
FSC® C105338

If you have any concerns about our products,
you can contact us on
ProductSafety@springernature.com

In case Publisher is established outside the EU,
the EU authorized representative is:
Springer Nature Customer Service Center GmbH
Europaplatz 3, 69115 Heidelberg, Germany

Printed by Libri Plureos GmbH
in Hamburg, Germany